JOY
COMET
IN THE
MORNIN

JOY COMETH IN THE MORNING

A Story of Healing from the Loss of a Child

FRAN C. HAFEN

DESERET
BOOK

SALT LAKE CITY, UTAH

Post your experiences of healing at JoyComethInTheMorning.org

Library of Congress Cataloging-in-Publication Data

Hafen, Fran C.
  Joy cometh in the morning : a story of healing from the loss of a child /
Fran C. Hafen.
      p. cm.
  Includes bibliographical references and index.
  ISBN-10 1-59038-708-2 (pbk.)
  ISBN-13 978-1-59038-708-5 (pbk.)
    1. Infants (Newborn)—Death—Religious aspects—Church of Jesus Christ of
Latter-day Saints. 2. Bereavement—Religious aspects—Church of Jesus
Christ of Latter-day Saints. 3. Consolation. 4. Hafen, Fran C. I. Title.
  BX8643.D4H34 2007
  248.8'66—dc22   2006030964

Printed in the United States of America
Edwards Brothers Incorporated, Ann Arbor, MI

10   9   8   7   6   5   4   3   2   1

For all who are "called upon to part

with those they cherish," especially when

those loved ones are children

CONTENTS

Contents

ACKNOWLEDGMENTS

I appreciate the invaluable contributions from others, especially those who have allowed me to share their stories and feelings and those who have given specific and meaningful feedback in earlier versions of the manuscript: Wendy W. Peterson, Audrey A. Richards, Monique S. Innis, Sarah H. d'Evegnee, Pat C. Higbee, Alta Batterman, and Bruce C. and Marie K. Hafen. I appreciate my parents, Ronald J. and Harriet W. Clark, for their tireless efforts to help me research and understand the gospel.

Likewise, I am thankful to the staff of Deseret Book, including Suzanne Brady, Chris Schoebinger, Mary Ann Jones, Michelle Wright, Laurie Cook, and Sheryl Smith. Their valuable suggestions, hard work, and beautiful designs have furthered this project and have helped to make the writing of this book a rewarding process.

Ultimately, I am eternally grateful for the encouraging and supportive heart of my husband, Dave, for without him and our wonderful children, I could not appreciate the greatest joys in this life and in the life to come.

Chapter 1

LOOKING BACK, LOOKING FORWARD

The warmth of the sunshine was surprising, despite the early spring season. The deep blues of the water provided a dazzling contrast to the white snow and the dark evergreens on the mountains encircling us. We were alone on the lake, finally free from the everyday distractions and demands of homework, piano lessons, and soccer games.

Our oversized canoe was filled to capacity with our growing family. My husband, Dave, and I were like bookends, safeguarding our seven children crouched between us. Our care to ensure an equal distribution of weight and basic paddling instruction were rewarded as the complaints of dripping water from the oars abated and our vessel began moving effortlessly across the water.

After several successful minutes of rowing, we approached the middle of the reservoir, stopping long enough to take in the beauty of our surroundings. Our son and six daughters were silhouetted by the setting sun that illuminated the tops of their heads. A strong sense of appreciation mixed with responsibility enveloped us, and Dave and I gave each other a knowing look: These are Heavenly Father's children, He loves them even more than we do, and He wants them to return safely Home.

Letting this moment sink in, I realized that my last canoe ride had taken place thirteen years before. Dave and I had been the only passengers that day, and the calm waters had reflected nothing of the storm raging inside me. At the time, only a year had passed since we had lost our first son, Devin, and I was struggling to acknowledge the wonders of God's creations. I had little hope of being delivered from my world of suffering and its accompanying emotions.

Looking back to my own first, tender encounters with grieving, I now could appreciate the meaning of "opposition in all things" (2 Nephi 2:11; see also vv. 22–23). What had started out as sheer torture gradually softened, and little by little Dave and I were able to look forward to the future again. Through the passage of time and divine assistance, I had learned to enjoy life again rather than simply endure it. I had come to realize that I could love others and I could love myself without feeling guilty toward Devin. Not only that, I truly could be happy, I could laugh at myself, and I could have fun again—as represented now by an exciting canoe ride with those on earth I love the most.

Furthermore, I now recognized that my fervent prayers had been answered. My doubts had been replaced with a strengthened testimony and a deepened resolve to rely on the Savior and the doctrines of the Restoration. Devin's life and death truly had been not only our most defining and refining experience but also a witness of how the Atonement had been manifested in our lives. Indeed, heaven had been transformed from a vague concept to a profound reality as we sought healing from the Savior and subsequently comprehended that "weeping may endure for a night, but joy cometh in the morning" (Psalm 30:5).

PART 1

The Story of
Our Loss

Chapter 2

WHERE CAN I TURN
FOR PEACE?

O nly weeks had passed since Dave and I had learned the cause of our unborn child's enlarged heart. After a lengthy ultrasound, a pediatric cardiologist made a sketch of the human heart to illustrate how our baby had developed two heart defects and how this rare combination might prevent our baby from living through the pregnancy or surviving the delivery. This report was absolutely devastating to us, especially after years of infertility testing and medication and particularly because we had sensed this pregnancy meant we had passed the trial of our faith.

In a matter of minutes, the anticipation of becoming parents was washed away in a tide of disbelief, sorrow, confusion, and anger—an array of emotions that we had never known existed with such intensity—all at the same time. I fluctuated between trying to be strong and feeling sorry for myself, and I grieved whenever I noticed other pregnant women, especially my sister-in-law, whose expected delivery date coincided with mine. Though I appreciated her warm friendship and her extra efforts to be sensitive to me, I couldn't help comparing our pregnancies and harboring feelings of resentment.

Possibly the worst part of our situation was that Dave and I weren't sure what to pray for, because in our hearts we wanted our child to be healthy and strong—to be "normal." And, because we often couldn't distinguish between our desires and the promptings of the Holy Ghost, we usually just prayed that we would be able to handle whatever we were given.

Desperate for peace and solace, I sought reassurance from any source I could find. But frequent ultrasounds from the medical world only confirmed that our son's condition was worsening, making his two options for survival a risky surgical shunt or a costly heart transplant.

Work and nighttime classes likewise became a temporary escape for me, but during the weekends I found it hard to remain upbeat. Sunday was often the hardest day of the week because the harsh reality of our situation surfaced again. Through most of our church meetings I acted as if everything were fine, even while feeling so terrible inside.

I often thought of the words of the young mother who had validated my silent heartache of infertility some time before. Afflicted with a rare and painful disease of her connective tissue, this woman recounted the time a friend at church had said, "You look so good—I can't believe you're sick." She replied that everyone comes to church in their nicest clothes and best attitudes because "we want to look good." Until then, I hadn't realized the poignant irony of wearing a mask of contentment—especially at church—despite a real need for support and brotherly kindness. I wondered how many others carried unnoticed sorrows because they "looked so good" on the outside.

Because I couldn't face others with such deep anguish, I was grateful that Dave was so willing to drop everything and listen to my concerns. As days turned into weeks, I continually looked to him for support. He recorded that he had "never known such heartache, not only for the life of our little baby in jeopardy, but also for my dear, sensitive, loving wife who has a difficult time keeping our son's condition off her mind. I'm sure it is much harder for her to deal with when she constantly feels the manifestations of that precious life inside her. In several ways it has been a blessing to us. We have cried and prayed and hugged and discussed so much over the past weeks that we have been drawn much closer together through this struggle."

Reaching out to Dave was natural and important for strengthening our relationship during our time of crisis, but I didn't realize I was draining him of his emotional and spiritual resources. One night, after he'd given me his all—which wasn't enough to fill my grieving needs—he drove me to the beautiful statue of the Savior on Temple Square and sat me in front of it, as if to say, "He can help you more than I can."

As my heart softened, I realized that my excessive dependence on Dave could become detrimental to our relationship. I now appreciated the answers my soul had ached to understand: "Where can I turn for peace? Where is my solace?" "Who, who can understand?" Because "other sources" could not heal my "wounded heart," I needed the Lord's "quiet hand to calm [the] anguish" of "my Gethsemane" (*Hymns*, 1985, no. 129).

Dave and I wanted to be faithful enough to reach the Savior's reaching. This lofty goal proved to be our greatest challenge, however, as everything seemed to depend on whether we could exercise faith and hope. In response to our pleading, the words of the Savior whispered to us, "My peace I give unto you: not as the world giveth, give I unto you. Let not your heart be troubled, neither let it be afraid" (John 14:27).

Though we had asked for His relief, we were given a spiritual prompting that was not what we had expected nor what we had hoped for. This personal revelation would become the most singular event in sustaining us through the months and years to come, but truly His response to our heartfelt needs was not what the world would have labeled peace at all. In a priesthood blessing, Dave conveyed the message that our son was very special and greatly loved by our Heavenly Father, but the reassuring words of "restored health" or "repairing the baby's heart" did not come. Instead, I was overwhelmed with the strong impression that our baby would not live.

My soul was wracked with incomparable grief. I thought of all the years of longing and waiting to become a mother, and my embittered heart simply would not accept the notion that our baby would die.

As we prayed that night for renewed comfort, Dave and I were assured of the validity of this prompting and the further knowledge that the spirit of our unborn son had important work elsewhere and needed a body for his eternal progression. This information somewhat relieved our burdened hearts, for we felt honored to be part of that great process, and we were grateful that Heavenly Father loved us, recognized our sorrow, and communicated with us through His Spirit.

We gradually became resigned to the idea that our baby would not live long—but *how* long his life would be, we did not know. Swallowing such a huge dose of bad news seemed impossible, but Dave and I felt inclined to trust in this spiritual witness and accept the Lord's will for us. We wanted to accept what was to happen, rather than ask amiss for blessings that were not to be. Possibly because of this approach to our prayers, the distinction between our thoughts and our spiritual impressions gradually became more defined, and the understanding that our son would not live long became the basis for all subsequent pleadings, divine guidance, and expectations for the future.

Over the ensuing weeks, Dave and I felt prompted to petition the Lord for three specific blessings: to have our son sealed to us at his birth, to hold him while he was alive, and to be with him when he died.

We had read that "although temple ordinances are not performed for stillborn children, no loss of eternal blessings or family unity is implied."[1] President Joseph Fielding Smith even expressed his "personal opinion that we should have hope that these little ones [stillborn children] will receive a resurrection and then belong to us."[2] Notwithstanding these comforting words, we wanted reassurance that our son would be forever ours by having him born alive. Sometimes, we felt we weren't asking for much, especially in comparison to asking to raise our son. On the other hand, we also realized that countless variables could affect the future and that many other parents had not been given these wonderful blessings themselves.

As the weeks went on, we were given confidence to remain hopeful and to do all in our power to obtain a heart transplant to further our baby's life, if he could live through the pregnancy. At the same time, however, we were also guided to avoid unnecessary heartache (such as scheduling baby showers and buying baby clothes) and even to discuss possible funeral and burial arrangements.

Most important, we were prompted to form expectations of what life might be like without our son. We attended special prenatal classes called "Unexpected Outcomes of Pregnancy" and learned the process of grieving. We were taught that we would continue to mourn for all our current and future losses: the loss of having a child with an unhealthy heart, the loss of being unable to take him home from the hospital, and the loss of being unable to nurse or hold him. We were also told that most people would forget about Dave's grief and that we should educate others—especially those close to us—by explaining which comments validated our feelings and which should be avoided.

Similarly, we were drawn toward others who had lost children to death. Dave's grandmother had lost an infant son many years before, and though I had rarely heard her talk of Jan or his unexpected death, I grew to feel a bond with her that surpassed the difference in our ages. When no one else knew what to say, she asked about our baby's condition. Because she had known true sorrow, I felt that if anyone could appreciate my heartache, she could.

One night, Dave's grandma spoke of the time her stake president had explained that she would raise Jan someday. After listening to her story, I felt safe discussing feelings I hadn't shared with other family members, including the impression that our baby would not live long.

Baby Jan and his parents

Maybe in response to her own situation, she observed that I was probably better off recognizing what was to happen, as opposed to not knowing and then "falling to pieces."

I replied, "Well, I'll probably fall to pieces anyway."

"Yes, you will," she answered with a soft and understanding laugh. "Yes, you will."

Dave and I later discovered an old photograph of his grandparents and their beautiful son. Taken several months before Jan's death, this image seemed to represent a bittersweet irony for all new parents, including us. Their eyes were filled with happiness, pride, and excitement for all the possibilities of parenthood; they sensed nothing of what would be asked of them in the future.

In the journal accounts of Dave's deceased grandfather, we read: "We loved our boy, perhaps too much. He was the light, the life, and the joy of our lives. We were so proud of him, we hoped such great things for him, he brought us so much happiness; we didn't realize it all, until now that it is impossible for us to have him with us here on the earth. We are going to try not to grieve too much over his passing—to live in our memories of him, to be thankful that he was ours this past perfect fifteen months, to get joy in knowing that he is ours, and that he will always be ours."

Preoccupied with these reflections of love and sadness, as well as the enormity of our situation, Dave and I were unaware that we were being guided through our entangled and challenging maze by specific personal revelation, for "without [it], all would be guesswork, darkness, and confusion."[3] Indeed, His promise of ultimate peace was being fulfilled: "I will bring the blind by a way that they knew not; I will lead them in paths that they have not known: I will make darkness light before them, and crooked things straight. These things will I do unto them, and not forsake them" (Isaiah 42:16).

By this time, we had already tasted of the full cycle of grieving: we had experienced the shock and numbness of our life-changing sorrow, we had searched and yearned for comfort and answers, we had felt disoriented and confused, and we had come to a sense of reorganization through the Savior's peace.

For now, this peace gave us enough courage to move on.

Chapter 3

SUCCOR IN OUR TIME
OF NEED

As the Lord filled us with confidence to take another step into the darkness, my scheduled induction day finally arrived. On a warm spring morning, our son was born without complications, his first sweet cries indicating he was breathing on his own. Dave and I watched as he was whisked away to be evaluated, and alone we pondered the significance of the moment: We had a son. A son. He was forever a member of our family, regardless of what happened to him in the future.

Soon thereafter, Dave and I stood by our son's crib. In awe, we stroked his small head and touched his tiny toes. I couldn't get over his beautiful dark hair and long fingers. He was nothing short of wonderful. Weighing an amazing eight pounds, four ounces, he looked so pink and healthy I had to remind myself that he was really sick. Again, I wondered how one could feel simultaneously so happy and yet so sad.

Despite the multiple monitors attached to our baby, I cradled him while Dave gave him a priesthood blessing and the name Devin. When the prayer ended, I kissed Devin's forehead and urged him on. His oxygen levels suddenly dropped, and as we watched the nurses rush him from the room, Dave and I realized we might not see him alive again.

Miraculously, Devin's condition stabilized, and he was transferred to the newborn intensive care unit (NICU) of the hospital. When we saw him there, he looked so fragile and yet so healthy compared to the tiny premature babies. An oxygen tube had been inserted down his throat, and because it bypassed his vocal cords, his cries were silent as he endured endless blood draws and tests.

Over the next few days, we took our family members, one by one, into the NICU to meet Devin. Dave's young sister was frightened to see Devin hooked up to a web of monitors and IVs. Not knowing what to say, she simply cried. When she later apologized, Dave reassured her, saying, "It's okay. We cry a lot too."

As Dave and I spent hours in the NICU, we grew more and more attached to Devin, and we cautiously allowed him into our hearts. It took us several days to comprehend that the little boy with the tubes, IVs, and monitors was really our son. One night, when I could not bear the thought of letting Devin go,

Dave took me to a private place in the hospital and held me for over an hour while I sobbed until I could cry no more.

The Sunday after Devin was born was also an emotional day. Because Dave was teaching a lesson in our ward and because I couldn't face anyone I knew, I decided to attend church services at the hospital. That day my whole soul seemed to be grieving our impending loss, and I realized as soon as I arrived at the meeting that I wouldn't be able to control my emotions. The opening hymn was "The Lord Is My Light" (*Hymns*, 1985, no. 89), and the speaker talked on obedience. I didn't feel like being obedient to the Lord, especially when I wanted to "will" Devin to live. I felt like a sheep stranded far from the fold, despite my previous belief that the lost sheep were those not attending meetings, not reading scriptures, and not praying every night.

My tears turned to uncontrollable weeping, and everyone there knew of my overwhelming grief. In genuine concern, a beautiful sister from Ecuador moved next to me, put her arm around my shoulder, and squeezed my shaking hand. She held me this way as I sobbed through the entire meeting. The Savior's light radiated in her countenance, and her sweet act of kindness somewhat softened my bitter, aching heart.

The meeting ended with "Families Can Be Together Forever" (*Hymns*, 1985, no. 300). I couldn't bear to sing it. Somewhat embarrassed, I thanked this sister for sitting with me. In broken English, she simply replied, "It is good to have sisters."

As I hurried from the room to avoid talking with anyone else, I retreated to a hospital corridor and waited for Dave to come back. There, I poured out my soul to Heavenly Father. I told Him that I wasn't ready to have Devin taken away, that it seemed so unfair for him to die when we were barely getting to know him.

When I told Dave about my experience with the sister from Ecuador, I realized that this was the first time I had allowed a complete stranger to mourn with me. She had taught me more vividly about compassion than I had ever learned from hearing a sermon or even from reading the scriptures. With nothing to gain by helping me, she had mourned with me—without knowing me or the reason for my sorrow. From her, I discovered that the Savior looks after all of His sheep, especially His lost ones, and I vowed not to forget the love she freely gave that day.

Over the following week, our lives continued to be full of emotional ups and downs. Devin was constantly monitored, probed, and poked, and his beautiful hair was shaved away bit by bit to find veins in his head for IVs. Finally, after days of many tests, Devin's name was placed on the heart transplant list and Dave was given a pager to inform us if a donor heart became available. Excited that Devin had cleared these hurdles,

Dave and I now hoped that Devin would respond well to his treatment and ultimately would receive a heart transplant and come home—even if he wouldn't live long after that.

During this time, family and friends made meals for us, did our laundry, and visited Devin at the hospital with us. Once, after hearing some bad news at the hospital, we drove home to find several family members waiting for us at our apartment. For the first time, we related despairing news to others before resolving it to ourselves first. Because they were physically there with us, meaning they were "there" for us, we allowed them to understand what we were really experiencing.

Dave and I especially appreciated those who asked questions and listened without cringing if we talked about anything related to death. One friend demonstrated this kind of interest in Devin and in us. Her inquiries were thoughtful and heartfelt. Instead of asking, "How are you?" she specifically asked how we had chosen Devin's name. Sensing her sincerity, I felt secure enough to relate sacred experiences and feelings to her. She cried with me, and she hugged me. Instead of trying to solve my problems or take away my pain, she listened. Her departing words were merely, "He'll be yours. He'll be yours."

Later that night, I realized that this friend's words had been most comforting and most appropriate for our situation. She hadn't tried to interpret God's will for us by saying that He "needed" Devin; instead, her words spoke the truth of our eternal bonds with Devin: "He'll be ours."

Likewise, my cousin Lynnae became a great support to me. When her infant son, Ryan, was admitted to the hospital for heart surgery, we spent hours consoling each other, convinced that the timing of his operation was not a coincidence.

One day, Lynnae presented us with a small, ragged, stuffed lion called Ryan's Lion. As we read the accompanying note, we learned of the lion's legacy for giving courage to others. Before it had strengthened Ryan and his parents, Ryan's Lion had given courage to Ryan's aunt when she had felt alone and homesick, far from her family. Before that, it had belonged to a woman enduring a painful divorce. And before that, it had strengthened a woman whose husband was terminally ill. Each person had passed on this increasingly tattered lion to someone else in need of courage, and now its strength was shared with us to help us endure our own challenges.

This tangible reminder confirmed that others were willing to replenish our store of courage. They were sympathetic to our pain and wanted to reach out to us, even though they didn't know exactly how to help. Their many prayers of support, thoughtful cards of concern, and gifts of service helped us to better understand the meaning of keeping our baptismal covenants: to "bear one another's burdens, that they may be light," to be "willing to mourn with those that mourn," and to "comfort those that stand in need of comfort" (Mosiah 18:8–9).

Dave and I learned in new ways that the Savior "will take upon him their infirmities, that his bowels may be filled with mercy, according to the flesh, that he may know according to the flesh how to succor his people according to their infirmities" (Alma 7:12). Thus, He knows how to "succor" us—to care for us—through the care of others. Indeed, we discovered the critical importance of what President Spencer W. Kimball taught: "God does notice us, and he watches over us. But it is usually through another mortal that he meets our needs. Therefore, it is vital that we serve each other in the kingdom."[1]

Our faithful friends, family members, and even strangers heeded the Savior's charge to "succor the weak, lift up the hands which hang down, and strengthen the feeble knees" (D&C 81:5). Without their overwhelming love and encouragement, we couldn't have survived our ordeal to this point. Dave and I had not realized until then how much the support of others meant to us, and we hoped someday, somehow, to repay others in need.

Chapter 4

FAITH TO LET GO

*J*ust as with all our past experiences, Dave and I could not anticipate all that Devin and we would face. The next few weeks were as emotionally, spiritually, and mentally difficult as anything we had endured in the past, and our faith was tried at a greater degree than ever before. At the same time, however, we were given divine strength to do the very thing— the hardest thing—we had been asked to do: to let Devin go.

When Devin was just a week old, we met with the heart transplant coordinator. He compared a transplant surgery for Devin to a man's bench pressing 250 pounds without working up to it. In other words, Devin's new heart *might* be able to handle the initial pressure of pumping blood through his narrow vessels, but it would have to sustain that kind of activity forever. Devin's pulmonary arteries might also collapse under this intense strain, and he could die during the lengthy surgery.

As if that hadn't been enough bad news, Dave and I were informed days later that Devin's heart valves were leaking. His window of opportunity for even receiving a transplant was closing quickly. Our spirits sank to an all-time low, especially when measured against the emotional high of having Devin's name placed on the transplant list.

Realizing that Devin's time might be short, Dave and I stayed with him as much as we could. Our visits with him were truly joyous, wonderful, and miraculous. Despite the sedating medication, the many IV lines, and the beeping machines, Devin responded to our voices and wrapped his small hand around our fingers.

We appreciated the medical staff, sensing that they treated Devin as if he were one of their own children. Not only did they continually monitor him but they answered our concerned questions and made our visits with him special. One nurse allowed me to change his diaper. Another collected locks of his hair and copies of his handprints and footprints as special keepsakes for us.

When Devin was ten days old, one of his nurses bathed and dressed him and invited us to hold him. It was the second time I had held Devin since he was born, but this was Dave's first and only time. Even though Devin was sound asleep, we treasured every minute of rocking him and taking family pictures and video clips.

Once, Dave and I spent more than an hour trying to coax Devin to open his eyes. Finally, Devin blinked and opened his deep blue eyes to meet us for the first time. It was a moment we would never forget. Somehow, it was like looking into his soul and discovering his pure personality, coupled with unexplainable spiritual wisdom and strength.

Absorbed in our visits at the hospital and our intense focus to keep Devin alive, we had a hard time returning to the "real world." Therefore, we didn't bother with unnecessary matters or events, nor did we care about the details in the lives of others, especially those involving the birth of my sister-in-law's new baby boy who had come into the world just a day after Devin had. I couldn't bear to think of her holding her son when I couldn't hold mine.

During a time when Devin seemed stable and healthy, Dave and I felt strong enough to attend our church meetings and face our ward members in testimony meeting. But as we listened to a number of people stand and talk about their children praying for "Baby Devin," we saw the reality of our trial through the eyes of others. Though we usually talked through our sorrow together, we simply drove home from church that day and wept. There was nothing to say.

The last week of Devin's life was a demanding and difficult one. After two weeks of apparent stability, Devin developed two serious infections. His body became swollen, his feedings were stopped, and he was given several blood transfusions. One night, after hearing the doctors debate what course to follow, Dave and I left the NICU in confusion. In the hallway, we ran into the parents of another baby who was waiting for a transplant. We had previously met them and knew of their child's heart problems. The mother related their current sorrows of traveling between two hospitals—the hospital where their baby lay and another hospital where her brother clung to life after a serious motorcycle accident.

After wishing them the best, Dave and I were overcome with a daunting gloom as we thought of all the parents who had children in the hospital. Every one of them had a story of heartache, and each had families who loved them and who wished they could take away their pain and challenges. This despair left a lasting impression upon us, and we arrived home emotionally and physically exhausted.

A couple of days later, we attended the temple with our families. There, I pondered the gravity of our situation and felt as Adam and Eve must have felt upon leaving the innocence of the Garden of Eden. They had realized they could never return to the peace and security that the Garden had provided them. We also had been uprooted from the comfort of our Garden of Eden, and our present life looked so serious and fraught with heavy consequences. We, like Adam and Eve, needed faith to walk through our own lone and dreary world together.

As Devin's condition worsened, his body became more and more swollen, and his name was removed from the transplant list. Overwhelmed at this turn of events, we prayed specifically that the effects of Devin's new illness would not spoil my brother's approaching wedding day.

The night before the ceremony, Dave gave Devin a priesthood blessing, in which Devin was told that he would respond well to his medications, be comfortable, overcome the infections, and qualify again for a transplant. This blessing stabilized Devin's condition and encouraged us to attend the wedding festivities the next day.

By the day after the marriage, however, Devin's infections had spread irreversibly throughout his body. We further discovered that Devin's kidneys were shutting down and his lungs were filled with fluid. We knew his heart was failing, and we felt as if our own hearts would break. Despite understanding his delicate situation, however, we were alarmed when doctors advised us to discuss options for Devin's life and death.

Leaving Devin in the NICU, we went to a nearby hospice room where we could talk, cry, and pray for guidance. Dave felt strongly that Heavenly Father was calling His son home after twenty-four days. But I could only remember the promise that Devin's health would return, and I had faith the Lord could heal him.

I prayed again, more earnestly than before. Peace came as I

was distinctly instructed that Devin had accomplished his mortal mission and that if I willed him to stay on earth through more medical intervention, I would cause him to suffer unnecessarily. This direction superseded the promises of the priesthood blessing, and only with this reassurance did I have enough confidence, strength, and faith to let go.

Dave and I were deeply convinced that we would not be "required to endure more than we were able to bear"[1] and that we would "have power to do whatsoever thing is expedient in [the Lord]" (Moroni 7:33). We therefore submitted our will to the Father's and asked the doctors to withdraw Devin's life support. Devin was wrapped in soft blankets and carried in to be with us. For over an hour, we rocked him and discussed our humble gratitude that we had been given everything we had asked for: Devin had been born alive, we had been able to hold him, and we would be with him when he died.

Finally, Devin's breathing became labored, and we held him while he slipped into the next world. In our overwhelming sorrow, we also felt a distinct and marvelous peace at Devin's passing. We were thankful for our last few moments with him and the knowledge that death could not change his place in our family.

Minutes later, our parents joined us, and together we decided to bury Devin's body that afternoon. Once the necessary arrangements had been made, I walked in a surreal trance behind Dave as he carried our sweet bundle to the mortuary car parked outside. Dave later recorded his feelings about this experience:

"It was hard for me to believe that just minutes before our little Devin had been struggling to hang onto life. It was heart-breaking to have lost my firstborn son, but I was comforted by the sweet peace of knowing that the Lord had confirmed to us that it was His time for Devin to return."

While being at the funeral home and dressing Devin's body was a calming experience, driving to the cemetery was almost too difficult to endure. Everything felt final—so irreversibly final—and I couldn't bear the thought of burying my only child. By the time we arrived at the cemetery, I was sobbing uncontrollably.

More than fifty family members were waiting for us, and as we approached them, Dave and I saw the chair holding Devin's small casket and the circle of crying faces around him. Impressed to thank each of them for coming, I reached out and hugged each person and was somehow buoyed up by a sense of comfort and courage.

The service began, and Dave and I stood close together as a violin duet filled the air with the soft strains of "I Am a Child of God"—a melody which proved to be bittersweet under the circumstances. On that day, in particular, we needed Him to "lead [us], guide [us], walk beside [us]," and help us "find the way" back to Him (*Hymns,* 1985, no. 301).

Afterwards, I gave the talk I had rehearsed for weeks, expressing gratitude for others' support, the gospel of Jesus Christ, the plan of salvation, and Devin's place in our family. I asked that no one forget him or what he had taught us.

Then Dave related the thoughts of President Spencer W. Kimball, who had understood that "the power of the priesthood is limitless but God has wisely placed upon each of us certain limitations" in healing the sick and dying. Had President Kimball had "limitless power, and yet limited vision and understanding, [he said he] might have saved Abinadi from the flames of fire, . . . deflected the bullets that pierced the body of the Prophet [Joseph], . . . [and] felt to protect Christ from the agony in Gethsemane." Dave also knew he should not and could not "frustrate the purposes of God," even though he wished he could have healed Devin by the power of the priesthood.[2]

After Dave shared our special experiences with Devin, his deepened perspective and testimony, and his renewed motivation to return to Heavenly Father, the service ended with the hymn "Lord, I Would Follow Thee" (*Hymns,* 1985, no. 220). Its words summarized our feelings in losing Devin: We still wanted to follow the Savior, to "walk the path that [He has] shown," and to be given the essential "strength beyond [our] own" to do all that we were asked to do.

The spirit of the day had been comforting and enveloping. Though extremely sorrowful, this intimate meeting had been beautiful and inspirational. In fact, my mother later remembered Devin's graveside services by saying one could not have come closer to the spirit world while still being upon the earth.

Chapter 5

THOU SHALT WEEP FOR THE LOSS OF THEM THAT DIE

The day of Devin's death was the beginning of weeks and months of aching, soul-searching, reaching, pleading, pondering, growing, and understanding. Indeed, continuing our lives without Devin was "a time to weep" and "a time to mourn" (Ecclesiastes 3:4). Without intentionally fulfilling the command to "weep for the loss of them that die" (D&C 42:45), we continued our mourning at a deeper, more intense level. Cradled by the faith and prayers of others, we found this to be an important season to remember Devin and to draw closer to each other.

The day after Devin's death, we purposely stayed away from church because we couldn't bear to face anyone. Instead, we read his short obituary in the paper and spent the rest of the day in the comfort of our families, sharing our pictures and video clips of him.

That day I also met my new nephew, Brian. He was so active I couldn't believe he was the same age as Devin. Brian reminded me of all the things Devin hadn't been able to do, causing me to talk to my sister-in-law about my pain rather than about her baby. Then, feeling this form of self-protection hurtful, I wondered if I should apologize. Because of my guilt, I held Brian for a few minutes, even though I wasn't ready to hold another baby yet.

The following morning, Dave and I chose a tombstone for Devin's grave and retreated to a secluded cabin a few hours from home. At first, I felt so apathetic and numb that I couldn't cry or talk about Devin. When Dave asked me to explain my first memories of Devin, I pictured him in my arms, his sweet innocence, his sense of strength, his dark blue eyes, and his small hands curled around our fingers.

The more we talked, the more angry I became. Everything was so wrong, so unfair. Why did we have to go through such an ordeal? Why had Devin endured such a sad, painful death? Why hadn't the doctors taken a different course in his care? What had we not done to prevent such heartache? And why hadn't we—unlike other parents—been allowed more time with him?

I wasn't sure where to direct my anger because Devin's death seemed to be everyone's fault and no one's fault, all at the same time. Devin had been given excellent care at the hospital;

we had done all we could to keep him on the earth. Furthermore, I didn't feel his death was God's mistake, and I certainly didn't blame Devin for dying. Nevertheless, I had to review all these questions again.

In addition to these intertwining feelings of guilt and anger, I was also enveloped with a gnawing emptiness and an acute pang of anguish, separation, and deprivation. My heart physically ached as I longed for Devin, and perhaps because he literally had been a part of me, I felt that part of me had died as well.

Even though we had been mourning our loss for months, this unexpected grief surprised us. We felt emotionally, physically, and mentally drained, especially upon realizing that nothing in our immediate future would bring us true happiness.

After we returned home to our regular routines, our grieving continued, now interspersed with Dave's school, my work, and everyday activities. Sometimes, the depth of my grief was too much to bear, and I avoided feeling anything in order to be able to deal with the smallest of tasks. One minute, I was dazed and confused; the next, I was furious about hospital bills or trivial matters at work. A profound sense of insecurity also encompassed me, for I realized I could not incorporate my usual coping skills of logically processing an issue, determining a course of action, carrying it out, and seeing the results of my decisions.

Moreover, every time I saw my nephew, Brian, I realized anew the past, present, and future impact of our loss. This little baby would roll over, crawl, and walk; he would grow up and go to kindergarten; he would wave to his mother in an elementary school presentation; he would practice the piano and tie knots in Scouts; and he would be baptized, receive the priesthood, and serve a mission. Not only would I miss those exciting events with Devin but I would also be reminded of that void every time my nephew reached another landmark.

During this excruciating time, however, Dave and I felt a transcending spiritual power, as if we were being lifted by the prayers of those who couldn't take away our pain. We enumerated the many blessings associated with our great loss, and we bore witness of gospel truths in our church meetings. I even recorded my gratitude for going through this experience to have gained a son. Because of Devin, I had become a mother.

Dave and I spent a substantial amount of our evening time together. Walks did wonders for our spirits, and Dave was always available when I needed to talk, cry, or sort out my emotions. At times, we felt so connected that we understood each others' feelings without speaking. Certainly, this special closeness was one outcome of our grief that we did not regret.

We focused much of our energy on remembering Devin. In his honor, we wrote letters to him and his future siblings, we planted a beautiful tree, and we compiled a scrapbook of his life, including photographs, locks of hair, footprints, and cards and letters from others. We somehow felt his life and death would not have been in vain if we could share Devin's life with others.

We also spent much of our spare time learning about "grief work" and the common responses of grieving, including denial, anger, guilt, relief, anxiety, panic, depression, loneliness, sadness, confusion, and difficulty in concentrating. We discovered that grieving takes more time and more energy than most people know and that it manifests itself in all aspects of our lives. Bereaved parents mourn for things both tangible and symbolic, including unfulfilled expectations and dreams.[1]

We read that our loss might resurrect old issues and unresolved conflicts from the past and that later in our lives we might experience upsurges of grief brought about by certain dates, events, or other stimuli. We further discovered that the pace and methods of mourning differ for males and females, but we resolved that Devin's death would bring us closer together rather than tear us apart.[2]

By looking through information about grieving, we recognized that others understood our loss and that our grief was "normal," even if our reactions to such intense feelings seemed abnormal. Like many other bereaved parents in our society, we had not grown up on a farm observing the natural deaths of animals, nor watched in our childhood homes the daily process of aging, nor witnessed anyone coping with acute and ongoing grief. How grateful we were that bereaved fathers and mothers shared their intimate feelings through art and poetry—all so that others would not feel so alone.[3]

Along with the examples of these strangers, Dave's deceased grandfather also became our role model in mourning. His beautifully detailed journal gave us the sense that he had not been afraid to grieve honestly, and yet he marched on faithfully, trying to make sure he was worthy to be reunited with his son Jan. Appreciating anew his sorrow, we read:

"I'm here in your little room now; it seems so empty without you. We wish you could write back to us, but you're such a little boy, and, somehow, God has not seen fit to establish any mail service between us. But you'll always know, won't you, son, that our unbounded love is with you to help you with your problems, just like we know yours is with us. We believe, little as you were, that you loved us, and our love for you is what is going to carry us over those years between. We want you to be a good little son, and down here, we will try the best we can to prove worthy of the heavenly little soul you are."

In addition to giving us understanding and comfort, the heartfelt experiences of others gave us strength to face others, a task that was harder than I had ever imagined. When I returned to work, I found that most people were desperately uncomfortable and even embarrassed when approaching me. I learned firsthand that the death of an infant is "not socially validated—that is, not acknowledged by society as an important loss to be mourned." Because bereaved parents represent the worst fears of every parent, they are "avoided more than most other mourners and are victims of social ostracism and unrealistic expectations. This is why so many report that they feel like social lepers."[4]

Many times, I wasn't sure how to react to the looks and comments of others, especially when someone who didn't know of Devin's death asked how my baby was doing. I carefully responded to these inquiries, first by reviewing Devin's need for a heart transplant to survive, and then by explaining his illness and death. Even with my cautious explanations, their expressions showed that they were simply mortified. Despite the initial discomfort, however, I appreciated *any* genuine interest in our situation.

Once, after I had gingerly explained Devin's death to one woman at work, I was shocked when she commenced swearing. She was furious that God would allow something so tragic to occur. Totally unprepared, I reacted silently with the same feeling: *How* could *God let this happen to me?*

Another time, a friend responded, "You know what I'd do? I'd get back on the horse." Though sincere in his advice for me to have another baby, his comment hurt, and I merely replied,

"Well, we don't want to have another baby just to replace Devin." Some time later, he apologized for trivializing our loss.

One particular woman had been a constant friend to me during Devin's illness, and though I anticipated this same sustained compassion from her after Devin's death, she merely gave me a big hug, said she was sorry, and walked away. She, who had heard all my reports of Devin's life, was never able to listen to accounts of his death. Her discomfort seemed to be another signal not to grieve—let alone cry—around others.

Things got progressively better, but many people completely avoided me or broadly smiled, as if nothing had happened. I didn't blame them, for before this time I hadn't felt comfortable talking to anyone who was mourning, nor had I understood grieving rituals and behaviors to be completely normal and appropriate.

Dave's work situation was the complete opposite of mine. Because he had just started a new job, he was surrounded with people who did not know him or his recent history. He was not reminded constantly of his loss, but he also did not feel support from anyone around him. Neither social situation was ideal.

Because most people could not identify with our circumstances, Dave and I greatly admired those who made an effort to say anything at all. The most comforting comments we heard were simply, "We've been thinking about you," or "I'm sorry to hear about your baby." We also appreciated comments of concern and understanding, such as "We don't know exactly how you're feeling, but we know from experience how the death of a loved one changes everything." And, every once in a while, someone brightened my day simply by saying Devin's name or mentioning that he or she had been thinking of him.

Although the first tender weeks truly were a difficult season for us and for those around us, they established an important foundation for future phases of our mourning and especially for remembering Devin. And while most of our friends—even those closest to us—wouldn't bring up our loss for fear of upsetting us, they were praying for our comfort and peace. Little did we realize that their prayers were buoying us up or that miracles would happen because of their faith.

Chapter 6

UNDERSTANDING DEVIN'S ETERNAL PROGRESSION

Throughout the first weeks after Devin died, we studied the scriptures and the words of the prophets to comprehend Devin's eternal progression. Although we had always believed death to be part of the gospel plan, trying now to deal with death urged us to understand it better. We reviewed the entire plan of salvation in relation to Devin's progression, and our hearts were softened and our testimonies strengthened by the doctrines of the Restoration.

THE PREMORTAL EXISTENCE

Our progression—and Devin's—started in the premortal world where we lived as spirits with our Heavenly Parents and spirit brothers and sisters. Because our Heavenly Parents "knew that we could not progress beyond a certain point unless we left them for a time," our Heavenly Father presented a plan to give us the opportunity "to develop every godlike quality" by coming to this earth "to be tested and to gain experience, . . . to choose good over evil," and to obtain physical bodies.[1]

BIRTH AND MORTALITY

Thus, life upon this earth became an essential part of our development. As evidenced by Devin's receiving a mortal body at birth, he had chosen in the premortal life to follow Heavenly Father's plan.[2] After twenty-four days, Devin's earthly experience and testing were complete.

DEATH

Devin's death was also a significant, purposeful part of his eternal existence, for "there is a season, and a time to every purpose under the heaven: a time to be born, and a time to die" (Ecclesiastes 3:1–2). Some mortals cannot be healed because they are "appointed unto death" (D&C 42:48), and we felt assured that our faith and prayers could not have changed significantly the length of Devin's season upon the earth (see Job 14:5).

We were intrigued that Joseph and Emma Smith had lost four of their nine children in infancy or early childhood. We took great comfort in the Prophet's words, for we knew that he and Emma could understand our sorrow:

"In my leisure moments I have meditated upon the subject, and asked the question, why it is that infants, innocent children, are taken away from us, especially those that seem to be the most intelligent and interesting. The strongest reasons that present themselves to my mind are these: . . . The Lord takes many away even in infancy, that they may escape the envy of man, and the sorrows and evils of this present world; they were too pure, too lovely, to live on earth; therefore, if rightly considered, instead of mourning we have reason to rejoice as they are delivered from evil, and we shall soon have them again."[3]

We certainly felt that Devin was one of the "intelligent and interesting" spirits, and in some ways, we were grateful he had escaped the evils of this world and could continue his progression in the next.

THE SPIRIT WORLD

Separated from his body at death, Devin's spirit now resided in the postmortal spirit world, for "when a baby dies, [its spirit] goes back into the spirit world, and the spirit assumes its natural form as an adult, for we were all adults before we were born."[4]

The spirit world consists of two divisions called paradise and prison. Spirit paradise is a place where "the spirits of those who are righteous are received into a state of happiness, . . . a state of rest, a state of peace, where they shall rest from all their troubles and from all care, and sorrow" (Alma 40:12).

On the other hand, "spirit prison is hell, that portion of the spirit world where the wicked dwell." For spirits in prison, "it is a place of learning and waiting; for some it is a place of suffering." These spirits "have not yet received the gospel of Jesus Christ," but they "have agency and may be enticed by both good and evil."[5]

Because Devin had died "in a state of purity and innocence which entitles [such children] to go back into the presence of God and have salvation," his spirit now dwelt in spirit paradise.[6]

Spirit paradise is a place of wondrous beauties, a place where "righteous men and women [are] organized in their several grades" and "family capacities."[7] Brigham Young taught that if we truly understand things as they are, we would surely say that leaving this world to go to spirit paradise is "the greatest advantage of my whole existence, for I have passed from a state of sorrow, grief, mourning, woe, misery, pain, anguish and disappointment into a state of existence where I can enjoy life to the fullest extent as far as that can be done without a body. My spirit is set free, I thirst no more, I want to sleep no more, I hunger no more, I tire no more, I run, I walk, I labor, I go, I come, I do this, I do that, whatever is required of me, nothing like pain or weariness, I am full of life, full of vigor, and I enjoy the presence of my heavenly Father, by the power of his Spirit."[8]

But "the spirit world, while a place of rest and comfort to the righteous, is not a place of 'do nothing bliss.' It is a place of activity and action." There, "apostles, prophets, elders and members of the Church of the Saints holding keys of the priesthood and power to teach, comfort, instruct and proclaim the gospel to their fellow spirits. The righteous spirits gather together to prepare and qualify themselves for a future day."[9] Learning this, we hoped that perhaps Devin would likewise be part of the great missionary work in the spirit world.

THE RESURRECTION

Devin's next step in eternal progression would be his future resurrection, because "all persons born on this earth will be resurrected" through the Savior's Atonement and Resurrection. Devin's spirit would remain in the spirit world until the time of his resurrection; then, his "spirit and [his] body shall be reunited again in its perfect form; both limb and joint shall be restored to its proper frame" (Alma 11:42–45). Devin's broken heart would be healed perfectly, his spirit and body "never to be divided" again.[10]

At the time of resurrection, Devin's infant body would be rejoined with his adult spirit. President Joseph F. Smith taught: "The body will come forth as it is laid to rest, for there is no growth or development in the grave. As it is laid down, so will it arise, and changes to perfection will come by the law of restitution. But the spirit will continue to expand and develop, and the body, after the resurrection, will develop to the full stature of man."[11]

Moreover, the Prophet Joseph Smith taught that through our obedience we would have the opportunity during the

Millennium to raise Devin—in his resurrected state—to adult-hood: "The mother who laid down her little child, being deprived of the privilege, the joy, and the satisfaction of bringing it up to manhood or womanhood in this world, would, after the resurrection, have all the joy, satisfaction, and pleasure, and even more than it would have been possible to have had in mortality, in seeing her child grow to the full measure of stature of its spirit. . . . When she does it there, it will be with the certain knowledge that the results will be without failure; whereas here, the results are unknown until after we have passed the test."[12]

But this wonderful experience can only happen "if parents are righteous. . . . Little children who die, whose parents are not worthy of an exaltation, will be adopted into the families of those who are worthy."[13]

This knowledge was possibly the most critical truth we had learned, and it became the basis of our striving to live worthy of raising Devin one day.

THE JUDGMENT DAY

Although Devin was pure and innocent, he would still be judged of Christ, for "all stand before the judgment-seat of Christ, yea, every soul who belongs to the whole human family of Adam; and ye must stand to be judged of your works, whether they be good or evil" (Mormon 3:20).

SALVATION IN THE CELESTIAL KINGDOM

After the Judgment, Devin would gain salvation, for "all children who die before they arrive at the years of accountability, are saved in the celestial kingdom of heaven" (D&C 137:10). Like other young children and those who are mentally disabled, Devin had not reached the "age of accountability," the "time when a person is held responsible for his actions," which usually occurs at eight years of age.[14] "Little children are redeemed from the foundation of the world through mine Only Begotten; wherefore, they cannot sin, for power is not given unto Satan to tempt little children, until they begin to become accountable before me" (D&C 29:46–47).[15]

Furthermore, "the infant perisheth not that dieth in his infancy" (Mosiah 3:18) and requires neither repentance nor baptism: "Little children are alive in Christ, even from the foundation of the world; if not so, God is a partial God, and also a changeable God, and a respecter to persons; for how many little children have died without baptism! Wherefore, if little children could not be saved without baptism, these must have gone to an endless hell. . . . Wherefore, all children are alike unto me; wherefore, I love little children with a perfect love; and they are all alike and partakers of salvation" (Moroni 8:12–13, 17).

As far as other temple work for the dead, "children who die in infancy do not have to be endowed," and "all that we need do for children is to have them sealed to their parents." Devin was sealed to Dave and me through our temple marriage, but "boys and girls who die after baptism may have the endowment work done for them in the temple."[16]

EXALTATION IN THE CELESTIAL KINGDOM

Lastly, Devin would be given the opportunity to gain exaltation in the highest realm of the celestial kingdom, which includes eternal marriage. President Joseph Fielding Smith taught: "So far as the ordinance of sealing is concerned, this may wait until the millennium."[17]

Elder Melvin J. Ballard explained that "even though some mortals die in infancy, that is no loss; no child has lost anything, for all the experiences that he would have had, had he lived, are only postponed. It will all come to them. . . . When we lost a little boy some six years of age I grieved over it, because I thought in my very sadness that he had lost something great. I grieved over it, and I thought, is it possible because of his death that he never will have the privilege of gaining that great exaltation? And the Lord whispered peace to my soul . . . that in the Lord's time, my son will have every right to choose a companion and receive the sealing powers that will unite him with one of his own choosing so that he can pass by the gods unto his own exaltation."[18]

Understanding Devin's eternal progression was very comforting and reassuring—for, as never before, we wanted the gospel in its entirety to be true. The Spirit witnessed these truths to our hearts, and we recognized more fully our gratitude for the Prophet Joseph Smith, the doctrines of the Restoration, and living prophets. Without these invaluable words and instruction, we would forever have questioned Devin's whereabouts and our chance to see him again. But the knowledge of his happiness and guaranteed eternal life gave us great peace, enlightened our minds, and strengthened our faith and hope in the Savior and his atoning sacrifice.

Ultimately, we realized that Devin's death truly had been "sweet unto [him]" (D&C 42:46). Because his eternal salvation was assured, death had contained no "sting" and the grave had won no "victory" (1 Corinthians 15:55). But for us, our eternal progression remained uncertain, and we thus vowed to forge ahead in this life, enduring our earthly trials so we could join him again someday.

Chapter 7

Lead, Kindly Light, amid th' Encircling Gloom

*E*ven as I reflected upon our newfound knowledge and testimony of the plan of salvation and our eternal progression, I found myself struggling to keep my head above the waters of grief. As if coming out of a daze with the hope that our understanding would neutralize our sorrow, I was now confronted with the finality of our loss.

Dave and I read about examples of faithful people in the scriptures and realized the important difference between enduring and enduring well. Resolving to endure well, I rediscovered the symbolic hope of the hymn "Lead, Kindly Light." Because my nights and days seemed "dark" and I felt "far from [my heavenly] home," I gladly welcomed guidance for my feet— even one step at a time. I also thought of Devin's "angel face" smiling upon me, and I wanted more than anything to live worthy of being with him again (*Hymns*, 1985, no. 97).

After a several weeks, we detected the weight of living on

our own spiritual resources again. Only then could we comprehend how the prayers in our behalf had upheld us through such a difficult time.

When friends and family members stopped asking how I was doing, I gradually became more withdrawn, concluding that everyone thought I was okay. But I was nowhere near being "over it." I wondered if others were too uncomfortable talking to us or if they had calculated our grief to be shorter than that of parents who had lost a child at an older age, simply because we hadn't spent more time with Devin or because we enjoyed fewer memories with him.

In addition to this, I wondered if our determination to be committed to the gospel had persuaded others we were "strong enough" to handle our difficulties alone. I even felt a need to maintain an image of faithfulness, worrying that if I revealed my internal heartache, others would perceive my endurance as lacking or my faith as faltering. Nevertheless, I truly was grateful for opportunities to testify of divine assistance and the plan of happiness, and I recognized that lesson preparations and heartfelt testimonies had been a medium for understanding our many blessings throughout our experience with Devin's life and death.

Sensing now that our support and "permission" to mourn were fading, I consciously resolved to be true to my emotions, something I felt I owed to Devin. I privately allowed myself to experience bitterness, anger, and self-pity without guilt. I believed there was no wrong way to grieve, and though I recognized these to be tendencies of the "natural man," I was determined not to torment myself for being "an enemy to God" (Mosiah 3:19) in my grief. I sensed that He would accept and eventually replace my resentment and jealousy with more positive emotions.

The more clearly I realized that things would not automatically get better and that my pain would not be taken away, the worse I actually felt. Perhaps because my faith wasn't great enough to deter or alleviate this suffering, I began to avoid helpful spiritual resources—the scriptures, good books, meaningful prayers, and insightful discussions with others. I consumed myself with projects at work, enrolled in extra classes, and escaped into a world of unimportance. There, on automatic pilot, I temporarily could be the person others looked up to, the person others thought was so strong, and the person others could joke with and relate to. But I was living a lie, for I definitely wasn't that person on the inside.

Even when I tried to pretend I was satisfied and happy, reality would confront me again. Life was going on for everyone else—a phenomenon that surprised me. School was starting again for some; others relocated to new jobs. Children were growing and developing. Friends were getting married and expecting children.

When my sister discreetly told me one night that she was pregnant, I was in a state of denial at first. But the news eventually ripped me apart, for I felt this new child would somehow take Devin's place as our parents' first grandchild. How could our families possibly remember Devin, especially when I was struggling myself to remember the details of his personality and short life?

To make matters worse, Dave's work schedule became so harried that we spent less and less time together. In response to the mounting pressure of performing well at school and work, Dave compartmentalized his grief, filing it away during the daytime and retrieving it only when it wouldn't negatively impact his career plans and our future family stability.

Moreover, part of Dave's grief was observing me suffer, and he sensed a need to be strong for me and to avoid adding his own sorrow to my burden. When we were together, Dave supported me by listening as I sorted out my fluctuating emotions. But, as I gradually detected that Dave had become more resigned to our loss and was looking to the future again, I realized how differently we were responding to our grief, and I sometimes questioned whether he was still mourning at all. He recorded:

"Time is passing more quickly for me than it is for Fran. I think we are reacting differently to Devin's death. His passing appears to have put a very black cloud over her head that she says keeps her from being truly happy. I must be patient and do all I can to support her as she goes through this difficult transition. I just wish I knew exactly how I can help her want to take the risk of having another child. There are yearnings within me deeper than I have ever felt to have children and to teach them the gospel and bring them up in a home where the spirit of love and respect is strong."

But I couldn't bring myself to think about having children. I wasn't ready to take *any* risks. I even dreamt of having a miscarriage and then apathetically going on with life—which represented how I felt inside: I wasn't "better" and I didn't care.

During one phase of my grief, all I wanted was to know if Devin's life and death had been in vain. As if forcing others to validate my anguish, I probed those around me to discover how Devin had influenced them. And just as I was about to explode that his suffering (and ours) had been unjustifiable and point-less, I learned of a special experience that had occurred years before Devin was born.

Approximately a decade earlier, my cousin and other mis-sionaries had spent the last night of their labors in the mission home. After sharing their testimonies, they had expressed their competing feelings of excitement for returning home to their loved ones and of longing to stay with those they had grown to love. My cousin was then given a distinct impression that mortals who leave this world through death likewise feel joy at the prospect of returning to their families and simultaneous sadness for leaving other loved ones behind. As a returned missionary myself, I could relate to being torn between two places and two different groups of family and friends, and I felt this was a poignant, powerful analogy.

The night before Devin died, my cousin had felt this same impression again. He remembered the details of the discussion in the mission home and similar conversations about those leaving the earth. Surprised to think of this experience after so many years, my cousin had then realized that our son was about to leave this world and enter the next one.

I now recognized that comparing a departure from this earth to leaving the mission field made death itself less disturbing—and maybe even natural. And though this was not the type of solace I had expected, my prayers were answered, and I was grateful again for peace and reassurance, through the care of others.

Gradually, the comfort of my cousin's words faded, even though I must have expected this type of spiritual experience to sustain me. I had to learn again that being blessed in our mourning did not mean our trials would be taken from us.

I acknowledged our divine guidance, but I never anticipated feeling so discouraged. Life hadn't been this hard when Devin was alive in the hospital or even immediately after he died. Little by little, I found myself becoming cynical and disillusioned. I prayed but not consistently. I went to church but not happily. Nothing changed my situation or my overwhelming feeling of despair. I had never suffered depression before, but I could clearly see the signs of apathy, unhappiness, and hopelessness.

Though I consciously had made no attempt to maintain any other relationships, I wished I could talk to someone besides Dave. Turning to my journal, I emptied all my feelings onto the paper. I recorded that I couldn't just "serve others" or "have a good attitude" to fix my world and that I wished someone could tell me that at a specified time—like eight months after my loss—I would feel whole again, I would live again, I would be happy again.

During this time, I was particularly depressed while attending my sister's out-of-town wedding. Dave's schedule had not allowed him to be there, and even surrounded by my entire family, I had never felt so desperately alone in my life. After continually praying for comfort, I felt inspired that Devin's spirit would be my companion that day in the temple. Then, although I didn't see him, I distinctly could sense when Devin's spirit was with me, as well as when his spirit left the sealing room.

Again, my needs had been met through an amazing miracle. Heavenly Father completely understood my sorrow, my fears, and my hopes, and I acknowledged the indescribable joy and gratitude I felt about being loved by Him. After I related this extraordinary experience to Dave, we turned to the scriptures to learn how we were being carried through such a challenging period of grieving.

Over time, we learned that the Savior offers us mercy and grace as the means of unlocking the power of the Atonement in our behalf. While the Savior's mercy is "the spirit of compassion, tenderness, and forgiveness," grace is the "divine means of help or strength, given through the bounteous mercy and love of Jesus Christ . . . made possible by his atoning sacrifice." Through the Savior's grace, we are given not only the universal gift of immortality and the conditional gift of eternal life, but through this same "enabling power," we also "receive strength and assistance to do good works that [we] otherwise would not be able to maintain if left to [our] own means."[1]

In reviewing our previous year of sorrow, we could not deny the mercy and grace that had been bestowed upon us, even though we hadn't done much to appreciate it. The Son of God—similar to the sun of noonday—had provided us light and life to endure the encircling gloom of Devin's death. The warm rays of the Savior's mercy had given us hope and comfort, and like the life-giving power of photosynthesis for a plant, His grace had empowered us with faith and courage we could not have supplied ourselves. Through His mercy and grace, we had been given specific, powerful experiences to answer our heartfelt needs.

Perhaps most important, we recognized that this same compassion and enabling power from the Savior could sustain us in our continued mourning—if we could just hold onto the "kindly Light" and follow the promptings of His Spirit.

Chapter 8

ANSWERS FROM ON HIGH

*L*ike feeling joy and sorrow at the same time, being able to develop spiritually despite such overwhelming depression seemed paradoxically impossible. During this season of both joy and sorrow, growing spiritually and experiencing deep depression, the very core of my faith was tried as I struggled to find meaning in my life and to understand how the gospel related specifically to our situation and to life itself.

Dave continued to support me by discussing my never-ending queries, but he was determined to be patient in our afflictions (see Alma 17:11), just as he had been counseled by ecclesiastical leaders. Although our approaches to remain faithful were equally acceptable, I desperately sought for answers to strengthen my wavering faith and to deliver me from the cloud of despair.

My first questions developed as I became acutely aware that individuals around me were suffering deeply. I met other bereaved parents who had lost children: a toddler who had died in the care of a baby-sitter, a fifteen-year-old boy who had died of cancer, and a young girl who had been murdered. I watched a friend lose his wife to divorce after he had climbed his way back into Church activity. On the news, I saw reports of famines, civil wars, and natural disasters affecting the lives of millions of innocent people. Indeed, suffering was everywhere.

Absorbed in this newfound outlook on life, I became overwhelmingly critical of those who didn't seem aware of this reality at all. For example, one night at a football game, I questioned how millions of spectators like myself could view such violent, nonsensical "entertainment," as opposed to spending money to help starving children in third-world countries.

Little by little, I realized that the most tragic part of suffering occurs when individuals choose to turn away from the only true source of help and comfort. After years of missionary and leadership service in the Church, a highly respected friend had renounced her faith when her first husband walked out on her. She was devastated that her prayers, obedience, and sacrifice had not saved her from such pain, and she vowed not to need anyone again. As she told me her story, I wondered aloud if she needed her current husband. That answer was easy: "I love him, but I don't need him." When I asked if she "needed" God, she thoughtfully replied, "No, I don't think I do."

After our discussion, I found myself filled with renewed grief for her and all the others who had suffered so deeply. I wondered why some people had not allowed themselves to remain vulnerable, having become satisfied with thinking they were "in control" of their lives. Why hadn't they followed the counsel to "continue in the faith grounded and settled, and be not moved away from the hope of the gospel"? (Colossians 1:23). Why had Dave and I been given such wonderful spiritual blessings as a direct result of Devin's death? Furthermore, why would a loving Heavenly Father allow or require so many people to suffer, especially when many of them weren't becoming better from it or turning to Him for help?

Now almost obsessed with a need to understand suffering, I found that others had asked questions similar to mine. For example, Anne Morrow Lindbergh, whose firstborn son was kidnapped and murdered in 1932, wrote: "I do not believe that sheer suffering teaches. If suffering alone taught, all the world would be wise, since everyone suffers. To suffering must be added mourning, understanding, patience, love, openness and the willingness to remain vulnerable."[1] Likewise, Viktor E. Frankl struggled "to find the *reason* for [his] sufferings" in Nazi concentration camps. He decided "if there is a meaning in life at all, then there must be a meaning in suffering," and he became determined to be "worthy of his sufferings."[2]

These perspectives reinforced my belief that suffering cannot automatically produce virtuous or beneficial results. I also felt hope that I could *will* meaning into my suffering and that the results could be positive and purposeful.

Notwithstanding this new focus for my grief, however, I continued to question suffering itself. I had endless discussions with others and became frustrated to hear repeatedly that suffering "builds character" or that it is simply a "byproduct of this life." I couldn't imagine God sending His children trials which might destroy their chance for salvation—all with the hope that they would develop "good character." I maintained that if the reach of suffering is so extensive, it must be a deliberate part of the plan of salvation. I felt that if suffering was not tied specifically to the Atonement, then our coming to earth was an incredibly horrible joke.

After weeks of praying and searching for an answer, I received a heaven-sent miracle in the words of Elder Orson F. Whitney:

"No pain that we suffer, no trial that we experience is wasted. It ministers to our education, to the development of such qualities as patience, faith, fortitude and humility. All that we suffer and all that we endure, especially when we endure it patiently, builds up our characters, purifies our hearts, expands our souls, and makes us more tender and charitable . . . and it is through . . . toil and tribulation that we gain the education that we come here to acquire and which will make us more like our Father and Mother in heaven."[3]

Finally satisfied by a message of restored truth, I realized that suffering, in and of itself, is a means of purifying us. Suffering not only has meaning but is an intentional part of the plan—without it, we cannot progress, experience joy, become like the Savior and our Heavenly Parents, or live with our loved ones again.

As the Spirit bore witness of this truth, I accepted suffering with its inherent positive and negative consequences. As Christmastime approached, I pondered the Savior's birth and His atoning sacrifice and recognized that because of His suffering He had given true meaning to all of my suffering.

With an increased testimony of Christ's role in our eternal progression, Dave and I felt our first Christmas without Devin was less painful than we had expected. By simply focusing on the meaning He had given to our lives, we found more meaning in the message of Christmas itself.

Moreover, my greatest Christmas gift that year was realizing an enhanced compassion for others. Now, I deeply mourned for those who struggled to know "Why?"— especially when the answer was simply "Because." I therefore became determined to serve those in need, a task I had not attempted since before Devin died. Perhaps because I was so out of practice, the thought of reaching out to others almost terrified me. I wondered if I could truly give of myself, as opposed to pretending on the outside and feeling bitter or resentful on the inside.

Despite this initial hesitation, however, Dave and I gave our little Ryan's Lion to my sister when she left home to serve the Lord as a missionary. Even though we still needed courage, we felt that giving it to someone who needed it more than we did proved to be very healing. As Ryan's mom had taught us, it was like laying something on the altar and walking away. While our "sacrifice" was not monumental, it demonstrated a small step toward willing meaning into our suffering and striving to become more like the Savior.

Once I discovered how the Atonement answered the question of suffering, my faith was renewed as I learned more about the true nature of Heavenly Father. While preparing to give a talk in church, I found that Joseph Smith had taught that in order for us to gain a "perfect and fruitful" faith, we must have a "*correct* idea of [God's] character, perfections, and attributes," for "if men do not comprehend the character of God, they do not comprehend themselves."[4]

I read that not only is Heavenly Father omnipresent, all-knowing, and all-powerful but He is also an all-loving, all-creative, and all-generous being who created the world "with breath-taking variety, beauty upon beauty, joy upon joy. . . . We are each unique and different—not to make life difficult, but to make life joyful."⁵

I then gathered articles about others who had struggled intensely because of their mistaken concept of God. For example, one woman suffered from low self-esteem that had developed not only from her improper conduct but also from her confused sense of God. She had believed that He was unhappy with her and wanted her to repent so that justice would prevail. When she realized she had overemphasized His justice and forgotten His mercy, she began to appreciate a more complete picture of Heavenly Father and her own self-worth.⁶

Another woman felt guilt and inadequacy as she tried to confront the consequences of having lived with an abusive father. As she faced the truth of her childhood, "the more difficult it was to trust God. . . . Part of me feared that this God, no matter how hard I tried, would not be pleased with me and could not love me back. After all, wasn't that the way my earthly father felt about me?"⁷ With divine help, this woman found that God "is perfect—perfect in his love, acceptance, patience, and support."⁸ He is indeed "a loving parent who patiently labors with his children, rejoicing in their triumphs and exercising patience with their weaknesses."⁹

Perhaps most important, I found I could measure my perception of God by evaluating how I felt upon saying, "Thy will be done." I read: "When you finally surrender your will to God, what do you really expect to happen? . . . It takes a lot of undoing of our conditioning to be able to say, 'Thy will be done,' and feel that we have just opened the door to moving in concert with a wonderful, loving Deity, rather than feel that we have surrendered ourselves to be cast into the fiery pit as a test of faith."[10]

Though I hadn't always sought to obey the will of Heavenly Father, I resolved to become more faithful and trusting of Him. I was grateful for an increased knowledge of His character and was thankful again for His hand in our lives and His care for each of us, individually and collectively.

Some time during my preparation for this talk, however, I received the negative results of a pregnancy test. Both Dave and I were now hoping to add to our family again, and we anguished over the possibility of waiting years—or never—to have another child. Worse yet, I didn't know if I could present the talk I had written, for how could I speak about a generous God when I felt so forsaken?

As I tried to identify the times I had received comfort and peace and testimony, I silently countered: *Why should I remain on the path of obedience if I am continually knocked down every time I faithfully try to stand up? Shouldn't I be helped to my feet instead?*

As never before, I prayed for a personal conviction of His

sustaining love. It took several agonizing days of pleading before I was reminded of the experience of being with Devin's spirit in the temple weeks before. With great power, the words from my journal testified of Heavenly Father's awareness of my sorrow and of His great love for me. With tears of humility and gratitude, I became deeply assured of His immeasurable and unconditional charity and desire to bless *me*.

Quite possibly, I could not have gained this abiding testimony without enduring some form of doubt myself and without subsequently experiencing God's infinite love for me. Only through such a powerful and personal experience could I truly appreciate and sincerely bear witness of Him the following Sunday.

As Dave and I looked back over our challenges, we agreed with a friend who said that death and grieving, above anything else, can teach us more about God, life, and ourselves. Certainly, I had discovered my ever-changing faithfulness and too-predictable tendencies to be thankful when all was well. When life was hard, however, I was easily susceptible to murmuring—despite all I had been given.

On the other hand, I also learned that Heavenly Father "is unchangeable from all eternity to all eternity" (Moroni 8:18). Though I had overlooked "the goodness of God, and his matchless power, and his wisdom, and his patience, and his long-suffering towards the children of men," including me, He knowingly had allowed me to endure specific and difficult situations, understanding I could become stronger and wiser by supplicating for His help (Mosiah 4:6).

Dave and I learned that "no matter how serious the trial, how deep the distress, how great the affliction, [God] will never desert us. He never has, and He never will. He cannot do it. It is not His character. . . . We may pass through the fiery furnace; we may pass through deep waters; but we shall not be consumed nor overwhelmed. We shall emerge from all these trials and difficulties the better and purer for them, if we only trust in our God and keep His commandments."[11]

While my faith continued to fluctuate from emotion to emotion and from day to day, I never doubted again the witness of the love Heavenly Father and the Savior have for me. Ultimately, the divine answers I received about Them, including Their character and divine purposes, lifted me from my state of depression, and I could testify that any amount of extensive searching, continual pondering, and heartfelt prayer is worth the effort to gain important knowledge and gospel truth.

Chapter 9

PERFECT LOVE CASTETH OUT FEAR

Seven months had passed since Devin's death, although at times it felt more like years. Much to our surprise, we learned we were expecting another child. But instead of providing relief to my suffering, this pregnancy revived and exaggerated my greatest fears, all during the time we faced the anniversaries of Devin's death.

With guilt toward Devin, I wouldn't allow myself to dream about another child. I couldn't even think of the two together, and it was rare when I had the perspective of them both fitting into our family.

When I finally went to my first obstetrician's appointment, I became so excited hearing the baby's heartbeat that I later entrusted a close friend with our secret. Even after she heard my tangled emotions and many fears, she couldn't see why I wasn't overflowing with joy. Exasperated, she said, "You ought to have a blessing. I mean, it seems like you're grieving more now than after Devin died."

Obviously, she hadn't seen me in the silent corners of sorrow or during the weekends when I had fewer distractions. Again, I wished others would give me permission to grieve. No one could remove my suffering, but ironically, others *could* relieve my burden simply by letting me feel sorrow itself.

During the pregnancy, the wording of my grief changed from *suffering* to *pain*. My depression was now gone, and my heartache was less frequent—but just as intense—as it had been in the beginning. Nevertheless, I found myself dreading all the anniversaries surrounding Devin's birth and death, and I wondered if I could merely exist for two months and *then* look toward our future.

As I had known it would be, Mother's Day was awful, but it was even worse than I had expected. My reservoir of sorrow burst open, and I couldn't stop the flood once it started. Attending our church meetings was difficult, especially as we watched the children sing songs to their mothers. When we returned home, we relived the memories of Devin's birth, his painful hospital stay, and the minute-by-minute details of his death. No matter how hard I tried, I couldn't stop the intense suffering. It felt like the scab had been ripped off a deep wound that was now oozing and bleeding again, almost as terrible as the first time.

Even though I acknowledged that releasing these emotions had been both healing and cleansing, I was struck with a paralyzing fear, worrying about other upcoming anniversaries. I was afraid of feeling extreme pain again, and I was afraid of feeling it in vain. I was afraid my prayers would not be answered immediately, and worst of all, I was afraid of forgetting Devin and of not loving another baby.

As Devin's birthday approached, I purposely decided to will meaning into the day, hoping to feel some form of satisfaction along with the anticipated heartache. Before Devin's birthday arrived, Dave and I bought a small gift to be delivered to someone in the hospital where Devin had lived. With this gift, we attached a poem we had written to commemorate his birth:

> *A Birthday Gift*
> *Today we celebrate the first*
> *birthday of our son Devin.*
> *He, like your child, was born*
> *into a world of suffering and pain.*
> *His short life underestimates the great*
> *influence and joy that he gave to so many.*
> *Devin's life was a gift to us—*
> *we remember him by giving this gift to you.*

But when the big day arrived, I was inconsolable and couldn't focus on anything at work. Finally, I asked a close friend, whose niece had recently passed away, to rescue me from my heartache during our lunch break. She took me from the building and allowed me to weep and remember Devin. After a good cry, I unfolded my fortune cookie and read, "We must always have old memories and young hopes." This message softened my heart, for I knew I must do both: keep memories of Devin alive and have hope for our new child.

Later that night, Dave and I delivered our "birthday gift" to a teenage couple whose tiny, two-pound baby lay in the newborn intensive care unit of the hospital. Though we found it hard to return to the place where Devin had lived and died, this experience turned a difficult day into a difficult *and* meaningful day.

Days later, I dreaded the approaching Memorial Day weekend, including the blessing of my sister's new baby and the birthday party of our one-year-old nephew. Although I thought I had resolved my resentment toward these two babies, the anticipation of seeing them brought me sheer torture.

Sunday morning, Dave was called into work, and I knew I would have to attend the blessing alone. Absorbed in self-pity, I found the journal of Dave's grandfather and read about the first Mother's Day without Jan:

"Dear Little Man: Today was Mother's Day. Your mother and I went to the Sunday School program. And even though you weren't here, they pinned a mother's rose on your dear young mother. A lot of the little kiddies paid tribute to their mothers. I noticed there were tears in your mother's eyes, and I knew why. Oh, little son, even though we try not to talk about it or think about it we both miss you so very much."

After the blessing, I gradually felt a sense of peace as I held my new niece for the first time. She looked into my eyes as if she knew me and all my sorrows. Likewise, my little nephew gave me solace at the birthday celebration. Six months had passed since I had seen him, and though I tried not to think about what Devin would have been doing if he were still alive, all my previous resentment was melted away by Brian's sweet personality and innocent smile.

The night continued to be challenging, however, even after Dave joined us, and I was too emotional to talk much to anyone, let alone sing "Happy Birthday." Later, we caravanned to the cemetery with fifteen family members. As Dave and I drove toward Devin's grave, I felt strangely as if we were on the way to bury him again—just as we had done the day he died. I could picture the spot where we had parked, the family and friends we had greeted, and the face and tears of my brother as he hugged me.

After the group circled around Devin's headstone, Dave related a poignant story of an earlier Memorial Day, years before Devin was born. Dave and his grandmother had been at another cemetery decorating graves as part of their nightly walk together. With her frail hands holding onto his strong arm, they had walked past a young couple cleaning the grave of a child. Dave had pondered the full life of his grandmother by his side and the life cut so short for the young child. The sadness of that scene left a lasting impression on him, but he never had imagined himself in the shoes of those young parents. Looking back, he was grateful for the endurance and strength of his grandmother who faithfully had walked that path herself.

When Dave asked if I wanted to say anything, I shook my head. The previous weeks had been almost unbearable, and I felt this gathering was only a formal show of sympathy. As if holding them all to a higher standard of emotional support, I had expected that they would have asked me more often about Devin or how I was doing, and I had hoped they would have come sooner to see his headstone. In reality, I had never allowed them into my private world of heartache, which caused most of them to be too uncomfortable to say much around me at all.

We finally climbed into the car, and I began to sob. I hadn't trusted my innermost feelings even to my husband. Only after hearing him talk about Devin at the cemetery could I disclose my harbored emotions to him. Knowing he dearly missed and loved Devin was reassuring and encouraging, for I knew again that I wasn't the only one still mourning our loss.

Because the previous days had been so tumultuous, I hoped that Memorial Day itself would be a calmer day. But when I discovered Dave wanted to play a round of golf on his day off,

I was outraged. Not even thinking he might need to relax from his demanding work schedule, I felt completely betrayed. I refused to go to a family party that night, and we got into an argument when he returned home.

Days after I returned to my regular routine, I asked myself what had possessed me during the holiday. I hadn't felt like such an emotional wreck before, and I couldn't believe I had been so irrational and intolerant toward Dave. As I considered the previous weeks, I realized that going through these anniversaries would have been difficult regardless of my greatest fears. But my reactions toward any real or suppressed anxieties had distorted my emotions—either by amplifying them to unreasonable and unhealthy levels or by suppressing associated feelings of sadness for Devin or of joy for our new baby.

Fear of feeling this pain again and fear of experiencing any future pain had caused me to avoid almost all spiritual impressions, possibly because feeling the Spirit always seemed synonymous with feeling pain. In short, if I couldn't face the pain, I didn't seek the Spirit.

Turning to the scriptures, I found that "God hath not given us the spirit of fear; but of power, and of love, and of a sound mind" (2 Timothy 1:7). Indeed, Heavenly Father hadn't given me this overwhelming fear, and the adversary had rejoiced as I had shut out the influence of the Lord—at a time I needed Him most.

I also read that "fear hath torment" and that "there is no fear in love; but perfect love casteth out fear" (1 John 4:18), meaning that fear and love cannot exist together in our hearts. I couldn't possibly feel spiritual promptings at the same time I was so tormented in my fear. Neither could I feel the Savior's love when I was so afraid to try, so afraid that I wouldn't be sustained in my new phases of grief.

I also discovered that "he that feareth is not made perfect in love" (1 John 4:18), and I gradually understood that I could not be purified in the Lord's love with my current fears. In other words, this suffocating fear would prevent me from realizing the enabling power of His grace to sanctify me and reunite me with Devin, and it could delay—if not prevent—further progress in the healing process.

Ultimately, I wanted to cast out my fears through the power of the Savior's perfect love. With His help, I could remember my divine worth and feel His unconditional love and desire for my happiness and growth—all at my own pace.

Thus, I resolved to face my fears, including how I responded to them and how they affected me. And with this renewed strength and hope, we braved the last of our anniversary days, the anniversary of Devin's death, which was also Father's Day. Without fanfare or fear, we spent the day quietly mourning and remembering our Devin and his short life.

Chapter 10

WAITING UPON THE LORD

With the first year of grieving behind us, Dave and I hoped life would get easier for us. I did sense a relief of sorts after we had passed through all the seasons without Devin, a phenomenon I later found was common for those grieving. But "a relief of sorts" didn't equate to complete healing, and questions filled the following months.

Halfway through my second pregnancy, Dave and I anxiously watched an ultrasound technician evaluate our unborn child. He couldn't see any major birth defects, and we left satisfied. If something did go wrong, we felt this delivery would not be as difficult as Devin's had been.

Though we were still a bit apprehensive, this ultrasound reassured us enough to start announcing that I was expecting again. Our family and friends were sincerely happy for us, and we cried tears of joy together. But often this excitement escalated too much, and I felt I had betrayed Devin by being happy without him. I realized again the need to keep my emotions from swinging either too high or too low.

Perhaps because I felt I could look more toward the future, I expected to feel consistently happy. But our heartache remained with us, and I questioned whether living the gospel could really heal my pain. We had tried to be faithful. We had tried not to ask, "Why?" We had tried to be "an example of the believers, in word, in conversation, in charity, in spirit, in faith, in purity" (1 Timothy 4:12).

Wasn't that enough to be healed of our heartache? Why did I still feel such sorrow? Why did I have to reevaluate and reconstruct my testimony every few weeks? Why hadn't I gained a permanent, eternal perspective that wouldn't falter every time a reminder of the past jerked me back into reality?

Instead of feeling healed, I felt profoundly vulnerable, vulnerable to all of life's terrible experiences. I had no guarantee of a happy life. How did I know that Dave wouldn't die unexpectedly in a car accident? How could I prevent another child from danger or death? If some experiences were the "will" of the Father or part of His plan, I had no control in their outcome!

My longing to be healed initiated another round of deep soul-searching. I questioned what healing really meant, for its process thus far had taken more mental, emotional, and spiritual work than I had ever imagined.

I asked Dave if he felt becoming eligible for the Atonement's healing meant first plunging to the depths of despair in order to recognize our true vulnerability to our mortal circumstances and our utter dependence on God. Must we be compelled to become *that* humble in order to turn to the only source of healing? And must we always remain vulnerable to life in order to be healed?

Furthermore, if I were healed, shouldn't I feel whole again? Without Devin, I felt that our lives would always be a jigsaw puzzle missing one central, critical piece. Feeling as if we had spent months and months in a frustrating search for this one piece, I now understood the awful truth that this piece was not only irreplaceable but it would not—and could not—be found for a long, long time. Would I feel unsettled all my mortal life that I could not complete this puzzle? Would I ignore the glaring hole in my puzzle, or would I focus on the bare spot as a reminder of how important that piece was to us?

Forsaking the hope of being healed or whole until I was reunited with Devin, I resigned myself to being trapped in my pain forever and to receiving only comfort and strength to endure it. In my heart, though, I wanted to feel alive again. I wanted to believe that life was good and wondrous. I wanted to feel joy and have hope for the future. I decided that acquiring this type of perspective would be proof that healing had taken place and that living the gospel hadn't failed me.

In essence, all my questions were tied together: "How long shall we suffer these great afflictions, O Lord?" (Alma 14:26). The answer we received, however, was not given as a specific number of days or weeks; it was about several important truths about patient endurance, or "wait[ing] upon the Lord" (Psalm 37:9; Isaiah 8:17; JST Matthew 3:24–27).

To begin with, Dave and I learned that this kind of waiting doesn't mean just sitting around and suffering, as one friend pointed out to us. It is an active and continuous faith: obeying the commandments, standing in holy places, and seeking direction through earnest prayer, fasting, and scripture study. It is, in fact, doing "all we can do" (2 Nephi 25:23), despite our afflictions and adversity.

We also found that "waiting upon the Lord" takes time. As with physical healing, spiritual healing takes time. For example, forgiveness and healing from the sorrow of sin demand a season of deep remorse, submission to correction given through the Spirit and by ecclesiastical leaders, and resistance to further temptations. Likewise, healing from the sins inflicted upon us by others requires time to process feelings of disappointment, anger, and grief, time to learn that the ability to forgive comes only through the Savior, and time to prove a continued dedication to Him.

In our world of convenience, cutting corners, and time management, I needed to learn how to wait—to wait upon the

Lord. In my impatience to become healed, I hadn't realized that a big part of my submission included being willing to endure on the Lord's timetable. In other words, waiting on the Lord did not imply that our road would become easier to travel. It just meant that we would trust Him and be willing to follow that path, regardless of the steep climb and the potholes and regardless of the distance and the duration it took to get there.

If we really wanted to arrive at our destination, however, we discovered we could be rewarded with wonderful promises of spiritual healing:

"Hast thou not known? hast thou not heard, that the everlasting God, the Lord, the Creator of the ends of the earth, fainteth not, neither is weary? there is no searching of his understanding. He giveth power to the faint; and to them that have no might he increaseth strength. Even the youths shall faint and be weary, and the young men shall utterly fall: but they that wait upon the Lord shall renew their strength; they shall mount up with wings as eagles; they shall run, and not be weary; and they shall walk, and not faint" (Isaiah 40:28–31).

Because the Lord "fainteth not, neither is weary," He is able to give "power to the faint" and increased strength to "them that have no might." Because I had felt so emotionally and spiritually exhausted for such a long time, I hoped almost desperately for my strength to be renewed, to walk and not faint, and to run and not be weary. If only I could patiently and actively wait upon the Lord, I would be given increased strength, even the strength to rise up with wings of eagles. Truly, my inherent longing to be healed could be realized only by waiting upon the Lord.

With this newfound insight, I earnestly petitioned for healing to take place. During a priesthood blessing, Dave conveyed Heavenly Father's admonition to continue seeking the Lord, for He knew my pain and He could make my weaknesses strong. I was blessed to know the uniqueness of our unborn baby and to understand that Devin was in the spirit world waiting for us. I was told I would be given more compassion to raise our children and to teach them the gospel, and these would be the most important experiences I would have as a mother. Lastly, I would be given knowledge and wisdom as I continued through the healing process and that evidence of my healing would be obvious.

As I untangled the pieces of the previous eighteen months, I again enumerated our specific blessings resulting from the death of Devin. This time, besides listing the blessings of a deep, rich relationship with Dave, a more penetrating influence of the Spirit in my life, and a greater compassion for others, I wrote down specific witnesses we had been given to gospel truths, many of which had come through talks or lessons that had sustained me in confusion, pain, fear, or bitterness. I realized for the first time that my weaknesses had become strengths as a result of our suffering and our waiting upon the Lord. These blessings were not only consequences of our faithfulness but also evidence that living the gospel truly could bring us healing.

Although the thought of having another child with birth defects lurked somewhere in my subconscious, I could honestly admit that tiny beams of happiness were breaking through the darkness of despair. I began allowing myself to think about the new baby; I considered baby names, bought baby furniture, and allowed others to arrange baby showers for me. With this gradual peace and comfort, I felt confidence in the future with another child—something I had not previously known I could do.

I was now grateful to understand the meaning of healing, but I wouldn't receive answers about feeling whole again until weeks later as we watched close friends endure their own trials. Their three-year-old daughter Jessica died in a car accident within twenty-four hours of the time when their son was born prematurely at an out-of-state hospital. As we shed tears for them, we were taken back to losing Devin and the awful, intense, and helpless sorrow we had come to know so well. We wished we could somehow protect them from the hot knife of grief they were surely experiencing.

At Jessica's funeral we were comforted and enlightened by insights from the meeting. In particular, one speaker asked,

"Despite our understanding of where this little girl is now, why are we still filled with such sorrow that it cannot be quenched by our knowledge of the gospel?" His answer was that our innate longing to belong to one another and the "homesickness" of separation from our departed loved ones are intentional parts of the plan of salvation. These yearnings can stay with us as a forceful, gentle pull toward our heavenly home.[1]

With this insight, we realized again that we could hope for healing in this life, but we also discovered we should not feel burdened to feel "whole" or "complete" without Devin during mortality. We truly could work on our earthly jigsaw puzzle without feeling compelled to finish it prematurely.

We prayed for Jessica's parents, for we had experienced the power of prayer in our behalf. We also spent time with them, discussing life, death, and the amazing truths they had been taught in just a matter of days. We knew the coming weeks and months would be painful and challenging, but we also had greater faith—for them and for us—that by waiting upon the Lord, we all could gain spiritual healing in this life as well as a restoration of all things in the next life.

PART 2

The Story of Our Healing

Chapter 11

INTO THE LIGHT OF HEALING

*B*ringing another child into the world was comparable to lighting a candle in a dark room. The flame was still dim enough that it did not penetrate the shadows in the corners, but its contrasting glow was definitely something we weren't accustomed to. Dave and I approached this transition blinking and adjusting our eyes, not understanding it to be the dawn of a new beginning—a beginning that would spread and grow over weeks and years into a sweet journey of discovery, growth, and joy.

Lauren's delivery was normal, and she was perfectly healthy, beautiful, and happy. Her arrival was everything I had longed for at Devin's birth. Friends and family members came to visit us in the hospital, and they filled the room with a reverence for new life as well as for Lauren's petite features, dark hair, and soft coos.

It took me several days to appreciate the wonder of such a miracle. When my confused emotions reached the surface, they paradoxically manifested themselves as anger toward those around me. The floodgates opened, and then I realized I hadn't expressed appreciation to Heavenly Father for giving us another baby. Subconsciously, I had feared He would take Lauren away, just as He had taken Devin. Sensing this, I felt terribly ungrateful and sobbed in remorse.

This form of rehabilitation finally allowed me to feel happiness for becoming a mother again. Dave and I began to see that having Lauren in our home was a sweet, exciting experience. We loved to watch her facial expressions and enjoyed parenthood with new perspective. We were thankful to hold her, feed her, bathe her, dress her—all the wonderful daily events we had missed with Devin.

When Lauren was a week old, Dave and I pulled out Devin's video and scrapbook to compare the two newborns. We had forgotten how traumatic life had been for Devin, especially considering how easy life was for a "normal" baby.

With pictures from Devin's scrapbook, Dave created a video tribute for Devin. Possibly, Dave now sensed more security in our future, for this was the first time since Devin's death that he had created his own grieving ritual. I was deeply touched each time I saw this video, as I felt an unexplainable support from both Dave and Devin.

Relieved that we did not resent Lauren for taking Devin's "place," we nevertheless did not sense that she was completely ours. We would not allow ourselves to fully bond with her or to think about her future developments of walking, talking, and going to school.

I realized as the days passed that I was suppressing deep feelings for Devin. And because I was avoiding my real feelings about him, I felt I wasn't being true to myself and subsequently avoided those closest to me. Perhaps I wanted to bury my past with all of its pain and frustration—only to learn that I had left behind a very important part of me. The shift of leaving the world I knew and "finding myself" in a new role as a mother left me feeling self-conscious and inadequate.

Some days, I had to pray to feel something, anything. I earnestly prayed to feel the spiritual significance of Lauren's blessing day. This request was granted, but the spiritual high lasted only a few days, and then I again closed myself off from feeling anything. Other times, I was surprised that I could become "selectively numb"—that is, shut out the sorrow while trying to soak up the satisfaction and joy of motherhood.

When Lauren reached the milestone of twenty-four days on earth—the age Devin had been when he passed away—I mourned anew. Shortly thereafter, I dreamt that Lauren died. In the dream, I was completely devastated, telling Dave I didn't know what I would do with my life. I simply had no hope of going through the emotions and physical struggles of ever having a child again.

Waking up from such emptiness, I was grateful the dream had not caused me sadness or anxiety. I was mostly interested that I had never had a dream like this before, because consciously or subconsciously, having another child die had been my greatest fear.

After that, I didn't worry that we would lose Lauren. In fact, I was given confirmation that Lauren was a part of my healing and that Heavenly Father had given her to us as a gift to appreciate the wonders of parenthood—without colic, defects, or worries—all while still remembering Devin.

I then began to notice I was actually feeling happy, and Dave and I discovered specific evidence that we were moving further into the light of healing. Clearly, the greatest proof of this was the ability to open our hearts again and love another child. And how we loved our Lauren. She brought such radiance to our home and such joy to our hearts. We celebrated her growth and smiles of delight, even when her satisfaction wasn't directed at us. I was content to be at home with her during the day and to watch her play with Dave at night.

We also found we were enjoying life, not just enduring it.[1] With a calm peacefulness in our home, I could sense I was becoming more mellow, patient, and gentle. I started looking toward the future with hope again and thought about bringing other children into the world. I even recorded in my journal that we would look back on this period as one of the most satisfying and rewarding times in our life.

Dave and I also recognized how far we had come in the healing process as we looked outside ourselves and witnessed others deep in their own suffering. One night, we spent time with our dear friends who had lost their young daughter Jessica six months before. Their newborn son was still hooked up to a monitor that tracked his breathing, and Jessica's mother felt that the complexity of their current challenges caused life to be harder now than when Jessica had died. We talked for hours about Devin and Jessica and the valuable insights we had gained in our mourning. Despite the incredible sadness we felt for our friends, Dave and I left grateful for the gospel and uplifted by their dedication to its plan of salvation.

The most conclusive evidence of healing was that our thoughts of Devin were mostly pleasant. Although we still experienced intense episodes of sorrow for our loss, they were becoming less and less frequent. Likewise, talking about Devin's life and death did not always bring sorrow or hopelessness.

Occasionally, however, just discussing our healing and happiness unlocked a heartfelt longing for Devin and Lauren to be together. Once, when Lauren was several months old, our built-up emotions for Devin came tumbling out again as Dave and I read a touching letter from my missionary sister. In it, she described a conversation with her companions about Devin, the Ryan's Lion we had given her, and their inspiration in her missionary experiences.

Her words validated Devin's sweet life and his influence on others, and Dave and I stayed up late talking and crying for Devin. Our deep grief returned as we completely reviewed Devin's past life. We questioned whether we had caused him more suffering, just to "buy" extra time with him. Had we had our current knowledge then, would we have allowed him to endure so much? Gratefully, we had no regrets: We had done our best, and we would have made the same decisions again, just to be with him and to give him every opportunity to live on the earth.

Intense heartache did not reappear again until months later, on Mother's Day. Hearing talks about motherhood was too much to bear because I silently compared our situation to others who were raising two children. Realizing again what we were missing without Devin, I asked Dave to take me home from church so I could grieve in private.

Devin's second birthday, however, seemed much easier to face than Mother's Day had been. Dave and I took Lauren with us to deliver a "birthday gift" to a couple whose baby had been hospitalized in the newborn intensive care unit of the hospital where Devin had lived. As we evaluated our grief over the previous year, we realized that we had experienced a handful of rough days, but it was nothing compared to the continual days of grief during the first year after he was gone. Back then, I had forced myself to feel sadness, emptiness, bitterness, and anger— just so I could function and go on with life.

Dave and I gratefully acknowledged the recurring effects of the Savior's healing: "For thou wilt light my candle: the Lord my God will enlighten my darkness" (Psalm 18:28). The flame of the Lord's healing had been with us throughout the previous months of sorrow, but only now could we appreciate its warmth and radiance. We felt confident that His light would continue to burn stronger and brighter in our future and slowly dispel the darkness of the long night of mourning.

Chapter 12

I NEED THEE EVERY HOUR

As we continued to feel the security and comfort from our healing, Dave and I gained a deepened appreciation for the Savior and His Atonement. Through several powerful experiences, we specifically learned that only with complete reliance on Him could we appreciate life in all of its seasons.

One night when Dave was out of town, I dropped off to sleep after a long day. Late into the night, I woke to an unsettling feeling of a dark presence. I became terrified, knowing that Dave was not there. Almost immediately, the words to the hymn "I Need Thee Every Hour" were delivered to my mind, and silently I sang:

> *I need thee every hour,*
> *Most gracious Lord.*

No tender voice like thine
Can peace afford.

Chorus:

I need thee, oh, I need thee;
Every hour I need thee!
Oh, bless me now, my Savior;
I come to thee!

I need thee every hour;
Stay thou nearby.
Temptations lose their pow'r
When thou art nigh.

I need thee every hour,
In joy or pain.
Come quickly and abide,
Or life is vain.

I need thee every hour,
Most holy One.
Oh, make me thine indeed,
Thou blessed Son!

I need thee, oh, I need thee;
Every hour I need thee!

Oh, bless me now, my Savior;
I come to thee!
       (Hymns, 1985, no. 98)

Just thinking these words forced the adversary to retreat and gave me the peace I needed to return to sleep. Relating these events to Dave the next morning, I continued to wonder how this song had come to me without my specifically praying for it. And while Dave and I couldn't understand all that had happened, we were given a profound gratitude for the far-reaching power and protection of the Savior and the watchful eye of our Heavenly Father.

This hymn became a great source of strength and comfort to me. I sang it when I felt down or when distressing thoughts came to my mind. Throughout the following year, its words continued to teach us how the Savior can bless us not only in our hour of need but in every phase of life.

Our first lesson occurred at the dedication of a new temple. By this time, I was expecting another baby, and our thoughts focused on the sealing powers of the temple and our growing family: Devin in the postmortal spirit world, Lauren on earth with us, and a third child waiting in the premortal life. And though no two of them were together, Dave and I felt a special closeness to each of them that day. We acknowledged that "no tender voice like thine" could bring us the peaceful reassurance that the Savior could help us to be together with all of them someday.

A few weeks later, I came to appreciate my need for the Lord when a close friend was rushed to the hospital to give birth to her first child. Her crisis caused my feelings of vulnerability to resurface, especially when I saw her son breathing with a respirator like Devin's and her doctor talked about the "tears that come when the mother goes home without the baby." I thought of our anxiety before Devin's birth and worried about my own pregnancy.

Thankfully, my concerns declined after my friend's newborn came home, and I rejoiced in his steady improvement. I recognized my sincere happiness for them as a huge step in my healing process, for I remembered too well the times I had felt bitter toward others who had complained that their babies had to stay in the hospital for a brief time, even when they knew their child eventually would come home.

Now, with the gradual healing of the Lord, instead of feeling so absorbed in my own sorrows—or even preoccupied with the deep sorrows of others—I gratefully felt I could "weep with them that weep" *and* I could "rejoice with them that do rejoice" (Romans 12:15). Thus, the "temptations" of feeling resentful when others enjoyed contentment or good health (or healthy children) had lost "their pow'r when [the Savior was] nigh."

Our next lesson in reliance on the Lord urged us to seek

Him to "come quickly and abide, or life is vain." One night, I had an extraordinary dream about standing on a plateau surrounded by several people. While trying to advance to a higher place where others stood with Christ, I wondered why we were different from those above us and why we couldn't join them, for I was certain that they were no better than we were. Despite my desperate longing to join this upper group of people, however, I had no way of reaching them myself. Then, realizing that the Savior would lift me to that realm, His realm, I was overcome with emotion. I approached Him, knelt at His feet, and wept with a reverence and gratitude I had never known before.

When I awoke, I was amazed at the spiritual power of a dream. Though I had always believed in the blessings of the Atonement, I had not remembered feeling so indebted to the Savior and so grateful to Him. This dream witnessed my heart-felt need and profound dependence on the Lord, for I knew in a whole new way that without His abiding influence, I could not progress further in this life. And, without Him, we had no hope of returning to the presence of the Father and of being together as a "forever family." Literally, without Him, life on earth would be pointless and in vain.

Months later, Dave and I learned through several experiences to rely on the Savior in "joy or pain." First of all, Dave went to the emergency room with irregular heartbeats, and over the course of a few weeks, he endured one evaluation after another to discover why he was having heart symptoms usually seen in older individuals. We were afraid that if some crisis happened when he was alone—or even at home with me—he could not be revived.

Our whole world seemed to be caving in again, and Dave wondered how he could leave me without a husband and leave his children without a father:

"This isn't supposed to happen to a healthy 28-year old. Our denial of this condition is slowly turning to acceptance. We have been silently and openly pleading with the Lord that I will be able to help raise our precious Lauren and her future brothers and sisters. In reflecting on past losses, it is certainly naive to think these things don't happen. I feel much the same way now as I did when we struggled with Devin. We must put our trust in the Lord and pray that we can accept His will. In the meantime, I find myself relishing every second with my beautiful daughter. She will always occupy a piece of my heart and I pray she will always have the light of the gospel to lead her every step and guide her through troubled times."

Eventually, after weeks of worrying and praying, everything slowly returned to normal. Dave stopped taking medication, and his symptoms simply disappeared. As we realized our challenge was behind us, our hearts were filled with deep peace and joy, a stark contrast to our previous anxiety and fear of possible death.

Not long after that, Dave and I observed again this same need for the Savior in joy or in pain. At the birth of our second daughter, Abby, we felt great joy and gratitude as we basked in the sweet spirit that accompanies the arrival of a new baby. In addition to this, we attended a friend's temple sealing and rejoiced in the celebration of a new life for her and her husband.

But our joy was overshadowed with sadness for another dear friend whose own temple marriage was crumbling. As Dave and I recalled her grieving countenance and compared it to the face of the bride, we felt both happiness and overwhelming sorrow.

Dave and I were reminded again that all of us—whether enjoying a wonderful progression or enduring a severe trial—must learn to "[rely] wholly upon the merits of him who is mighty to save" (2 Nephi 31:19). In opposing situations—health and sickness, marriage and divorce, life and death—only He can bring us real joy, and only He can truly heal us of our pain.

Lastly, through the events surrounding the death of Dave's grandmother, Dave and I were taught one more reason to need the Savior. By then it had been over three years since Devin had passed away, and I wondered how I would react toward the death of a family member—even though Dave's grandmother had grown more and more ill and we knew her time was short. A few nights before her passing, we said our last good-byes at her bedside and reflected on her life. I thought of the sorrow she and her husband had felt at the death of their son Jan, and I truly rejoiced for them for their upcoming and glorious reunion, as had been anticipated in her husband's journal many decades before:

"In a few short years, we will be old, and ready to go on to newer and greater experiences. What a joy it will be to meet our son again. And until that happy day, we want to live in our memories of him; we want our faith to be strengthened, our lives to be made bigger and better. God bless and sanctify his memory, and help us to understand His infinite purposes in all things."

Because of this comfort, I didn't expect to feel such sadness when I learned that Dave's grandmother had passed away. We arrived at the hospital minutes after she died and were enveloped by the sweet and peaceful spirit that attends the sacred experience of leaving this life and entering the next.

The funeral for Dave's grandma was uplifting, and we left feeling inspired to become better people, wanting never to settle for mediocrity in our lives. She had lived a full and faithful life, and in her memory, Dave and I transplanted two of her beautiful rose bushes into our garden to remind us of her dedication to the Savior and our eternal potential to bloom in His care.

Again, the words of the hymn came to my mind:

> *I need thee every hour,*
> *Most holy One.*
> *Oh, make me thine indeed,*
> *Thou blessed Son!*

Dave's grandmother had understood her need for the Savior, and ultimately her lifelong dependence upon Him had helped her to become His spiritual daughter indeed.

Perhaps her triumph and advancement to the next world meant even more to us than just releasing a mortal being from her illness, sorrows, and cares. Sensing that one of our greatest role models in grieving had conquered the world through her faithfulness was a kind of victory for us. We were convinced that her efforts, as well as the efforts of her husband, had paid off, and we had great hope that ours would be rewarded as well.

The lessons of "I need Thee every hour" would continually remind us to rely upon the Savior and His atoning sacrifice. Hour by hour and moment by moment, we need His tender voice and His lasting peace. In good times and in bad, we need Him nearby to help us overcome temptation and to reassure us that our earthly existence will not be in vain. Only our complete reliance upon Him can assist us in becoming His spiritual sons and daughters, now and in the eternities.

Chapter 13

MOURNING WITH THOSE THAT MOURN

*D*uring our earlier trials, Dave and I had appreciated the prayers and support from our family and friends. Then, as life became more stable and predictable, we started to reach out to others. Each sweet and memorable experience with those in need taught us about fulfilling our baptismal covenants to be "willing to mourn with those that mourn," "to bear one another's burdens, that they may be light," and to "comfort those that stand in need of comfort" (Mosiah 18:8–9).

When we learned that someone had lost a child, Dave and I sent copies of the grieving materials that had been so valuable to us, and we combed the toy stores to find stuffed Ryan's Lions to give them courage. We wrote letters, made phone calls, and spent time talking about our losses.

For the first time I grieved with a young mother I had not met before. Our conversation initially seemed a little forced and formal, but gradually we felt comfortable expressing our deepest feelings to one another. Not only did I sorrow over the loss of her daughter, Breanna, but I also relived my own sadness. And though these reminders were painful, I was grateful to truly mourn with her as a way of remembering and respecting Devin.

That day, I appreciated anew the special kinship that occurs when people grieve together. In a matter of hours, two strangers were bonded as close friends by sharing intimate experiences, heartache, and hope. After such a short time, I felt I had known her all my life and could tell her anything in my heart. It had taken me years to open up to others, but as I had tried to comfort her, she, in turn, provided me with a safe haven to communicate my own tender feelings.

Furthermore, I recognized that I never could have tasted of that sacred experience without having lost Devin first. Because of my own past suffering and healing, I could help others— even complete strangers—to feel validated in their sorrow and to feel hope for the future.

Little by little, Dave and I then initiated conversations with people enduring difficult trials as they fell prey to the adversary's subtleties. We sensed the common thread of suffering and the need for healing from the Atonement. We knew that the enabling grace of the Savior could make up for all weaknesses and these individuals could become stable, secure, and happy.

Likewise, because we recognized that our grieving had been a process, we knew of their constant need for support through the repentance process.

Sharing such intimate, sacred experiences and feelings with others ranked among some of our most spiritual experiences. They became the means of learning many truths and of clarifying our own growth.

For example, while I was recovering from a miscarriage and its accompanying emotions of emptiness, devastation, and vulnerability, Dave and I discovered another reason to grieve. Our friend and neighbor, Marc, was diagnosed with cancer of the esophagus and stomach, and he and his young wife, Carol, were completely overwhelmed at the news. Although our heartache at the time was completely different, our trials brought us closer as friends, and we talked with them for hours about life and death, the gospel, and their hopes and fears for the future.

Just weeks before Christmas, Marc endured a rough surgery, only to learn that the cancer had spread to his lymph nodes and that he would live only twelve to eighteen months longer. The holidays seemed hopelessly heavy with sorrow, and we couldn't bear to think of Marc dying or of Carol raising three small boys alone.

In the ensuing weeks, while Marc struggled just to exist with constant nausea and pain, he and Carol felt close friends pull away. Because of our past experiences, Dave and I were grateful to somehow help them as they now faced Marc's death. We even wondered if Dave's previous heart problems and our associated vulnerability to his possible death had been a means of preparing us to support them.

Nineteen months after his diagnosis, Marc was moved to a hospice facility and given heavy doses of medication for pain relief. Carol explained that Marc's death was imminent and that she needed to get things ready for his funeral. When I offered to help, she asked me to purchase Marc's burial clothes. After agreeing to do this, however, I thought of all the things I needed to do and wondered if I should just take care of this errand during a more convenient time. Suddenly, I realized that all my busy tasks that day were pointless and trivial.

After canceling my plans and loading the kids into the car, I was inspired that my trip was not about buying clothes for Marc; it was about supporting Carol. The Spirit then whispered that Marc's last day on earth would be that very day.

Because I had listened to these promptings, I was able to say good-bye to Marc before he died that afternoon. I was also able to witness the exchange between Carol and a hospice center employee, who knelt beside her and said, "I want you to know it has been an absolute privilege to work with your husband." Because I had listened, I had been one more friend who was "there" for Carol as she braved one of the toughest days of her life.

At Marc's funeral, Dave and I reminisced about all of Marc's endearing qualities: his quick wit, his allegiance to the Savior, his loyalty to his family, and his example of focusing on others rather than on himself.

We left the cemetery feeling humbled to have learned that the charge to "comfort yourselves together, and edify one another" through exhorting, consoling, and encouraging (1 Thessalonians 5:11; footnote 11*a*) is a sacred trust and a special opportunity that must be taken whenever the Spirit prompts us.

We also knew Carol faced a long and difficult road, and we resolved to stay close to her, especially when the time came that others less directly acquainted with such losses would feel she should be over Marc's death.

Not long after Marc's funeral, Dave and I participated in another tender learning experience of mourning with those that mourn. We were overcome with great sadness to learn that a couple in our ward had lost their sixteen-month-old daughter, Jaclyn, in a drowning accident. We had always been drawn to this family and their conscious efforts to serve and lift others. At the viewing, Jaclyn's mother, Maureen, warmly approached us and said, "I thought we would only have to experience this once." They had already lost their first child, Jaclyn's older brother, who had died at birth. I reflected on these words again and again, and I wondered what I would do if I ever lost another child.

The next day, Dave and I were deeply touched by the messages at Jaclyn's funeral, and we were consoled to hear that Jaclyn would be aware not only of her family's heartaches and loneliness but also of their birthdays, baptisms, graduations, and sealing ordinances. More important, though, she would know of her family's mortal progression in qualifying to be with her again.

Six months after Jaclyn's death, as the Christmas holidays approached, I felt prompted to write Maureen during this difficult time without Jaclyn:

"I don't know if I will ever feel completely whole again without Devin. He is still such a part of our lives and our family. But I can honestly say I don't grieve over his loss—only at certain times. His memory mostly brings me joy—not the deep pain of the past. And in some strange way, Dave and I feel grateful for our experience of losing Devin. We are different people and different parents now because of his death."

Expressing gratitude for Devin's death was surprising, if not eye-opening, for me. I had always described only the wonderful blessings resulting from his death. But honestly admitting that I was thankful it had happened was evidence of healing and undeniable acceptance and understanding of our sorrow.

Later that spring, Dave and I had the opportunity to travel

out of the country where we learned about a couple who had recently lost a baby. I felt an urgency to meet the mother that day, rather than just writing her or calling her from home.

We later found Monique to be a person whose countenance radiated a light and whose bright smile didn't always reveal her deep sorrow. After we described our little Devin, his heart defects, and his death, Monique showed us pictures of her thirteen-week-old Benjamin and explained the rare viral carditis that took his life in just two days.

Over the course of our discussion, Dave and I were amazed to recall stories and emotions we hadn't thought about for months and years. As we listened to Monique, we were directed to relate specific experiences that validated her grief and answered her questions.

Dave and I learned from Monique more about our own blessings associated with Devin's death. For example, when Monique honestly explained to us how difficult it was to watch her husband bless Benjamin to be released from his suffering, we realized that we had been able to submit our wills to Heavenly Father's will—we had felt a sense of ownership in the decision to let Devin die. Not recognizing this as a blessing before, we concluded that our opportunity to submit humbly must have softened the bitterness we felt toward Heavenly Father after Devin's death. We also wondered if He sometimes allows the dying to tarry on the earth—and maybe suffer longer—so that their loved ones feel reconciled to the death and experience ownership in the decision to let the dying individual return Home.

The entire conversation with Monique was sorrowful, yet amazingly uplifting. When it was time to leave, she thanked us for enabling her to express bottled-up emotions. We were humbled to be allowed into her heart, especially after hearing her relate the question she had asked herself that very morning: "Why won't anyone talk to me about this?"

That night was the beginning of a wonderful friendship, and we stayed in touch with Monique after we came home. I mailed her a Ryan's Lion, grieving information, and copies of certain journal entries. I was prompted to write that Benjamin was acutely aware of her and that he loved her in a very real and profound way.

After several months, Monique and her husband came to visit us. While this was a sweet reunion, the highlight for me was introducing Monique to Maureen. Although Maureen was still grieving eighteen months after Jaclyn's death, the overshadowing despair was lifting. She could now appreciate the effects of the Savior's healing and could extend encouragement and hope to Monique.

As an almost silent witness of their conversation, I realized that because Maureen was just months ahead of Monique in her own grief, she could offer Monique what I could not give.

As I listened to them express tender feelings and observed their progress toward understanding, compassion, warmth, and hope, I felt I was standing on holy ground (see Exodus 3:5). Indeed, this marvelous experience was a powerful manifestation of the Atonement in both their lives and mine.

Later, Dave and I compared this experience to that of Alma the Younger. When Alma witnessed others who had endured trials similar to his own "coming to the Lord their God, then is my soul filled with joy; then do I remember what the Lord has done for me, yea, even that he hath heard my prayer; yea, then do I remember his merciful arm which he extended towards me" (Alma 29:10).

Indeed, healing from any loss cannot be complete until we reach out to those in need and until we specifically realize what divine help we have been given in our own lives. And sometimes, we can't comprehend what we have been given until we see that heavenly grace manifested in the lives of others.

Chapter 14

SWEET ABOVE ALL
THAT IS SWEET

As our lives filled with the responsibilities of raising our young children, Dave and I found that the Lord placed significantly fewer experiences of "mourning with those that mourn" in our path. While we tried not to turn down any opportunities to serve those who were suffering, our efforts gradually shifted toward caring for our growing family. Despite an often steep parental learning curve, we experienced joy and satisfaction, and over several years we uncovered a priceless treasure: the meaning of sweet and eternal relationships with one another and with Devin.

When Devin had been gone more than six years, I was asked to speak at the funeral of my paternal grandmother. Consciously inadequate, I felt I just couldn't do it. I hadn't been very supportive of her needs, and I recognized that others could speak more eloquently about her life. Worse yet, because my grandma had been adversely affected by the process of aging and memory loss, I didn't know her very well at all.

Despite that, I consented to the task and was given seventeen pages of Grandma's history, written in her beautiful handwriting. Fascinated, I read about Grandma's childhood, her conversion to the Church, her forty years of family history and temple work, and her last act of service to her husband before he died.

Though Grandma's history did not express the heartache she felt at Grandpa's passing, I was filled with an unexplainable and overwhelming grief—a taste of what Grandma had suffered during her great loss. It was as though I was mourning with her, even though Grandpa had passed away decades before and even though Grandma had already joined him in the spirit world.

While pondering this extraordinary experience later, I was prompted that I had been given an outpouring of the spirit of Elijah in turning my heart toward my grandmother. Somehow, by identifying with her sorrow, I was given a great appreciation and love for her—more than I could have acquired simply by reading her record. With this divine help, I perceived her faithfulness in times of tribulation, her abiding love for her family, and her quiet devotion and selflessness that had welded thousands of our family members to one another.

In just a few days, Grandma had become my hero. With renewed admiration for her, I was inspired to speak about how the spirit of Elijah had motivated her throughout her life. I resolved to follow her example of staying spiritually "linked" by fostering eternal relationships with those in our family chain.

This experience taught Dave and me that the spirit of Elijah involves more than just an inner drive to do temple ordinances for our ancestors—it includes powerful yearnings to become welded together in love to our families on both sides of the veil (Malachi 4:5–6).

President James E. Faust said: "Perhaps we regard the power bestowed by Elijah as something associated only with formal ordinances performed in sacred places. But these ordinances become dynamic and productive of good only as they reveal themselves in our daily lives. Malachi said that the power of Elijah would turn the hearts of the fathers and the children to each other. . . . This sealing power thus reveals itself in family relationships, in attributes and virtues developed in a nurturing environment, and in loving service. These are the cords that bind families together."[1]

Therefore, the purpose of having Elijah return was first to provide the necessary keys to seal families together and then to help those family members return safely Home *together.* Just as Grandma had felt compelled by the spirit of Elijah to search out her kindred dead, so we could be inspired to sacrifice specifically for the people we hoped to be with in the eternities.

Possibly it was the spirit of Elijah that had drawn Dave and me together as husband and wife throughout our period of grieving. And the spirit of Elijah likely had motivated us in numerous ways to improve our relationships with our children, such as directing us to learn the importance of good parenting skills, putting our family's needs above all other demands on our time, disciplining while keeping loving relationships intact, and teaching our children their great worth and our hopes to be with them forever.

If this were the case, the spirit of Elijah surely would continue to inspire us to maintain our relationships during challenging times and to repair and rekindle those relationships after the crises had settled.

As I envisioned the lives of our family members becoming meshed together on earth, however, I realized that through the spirit of Elijah our eternal relationships and friendships could become much more than this. I thought about the wonderful times in our marriage when Dave and I were in sync with our marital goals, our parenting efforts, and our focus on the gospel, and I could not deny feeling an emotional and spiritual connectedness to him. Certainly, this was the way I envisioned a solid marriage—now and throughout eternity.

Then I considered the precious moments when peace and harmony permeated our home. These were the times when Dave and I remembered our children's divine heritage and potential, recognizing who they were becoming rather than what they had not accomplished.

These were the times when our children were respectful and willing to work together as a family and when our home was a safe haven from the world, a place where we enjoyed being together. These were the times when "there was no contention in the land, because of the love of God which did dwell in the hearts of the people . . . and surely there could not be a happier people" (4 Nephi 1:15–16).

As Dave and I analyzed our relationships during these moments, we compared them to tasting the fruit described as the "most precious, which is sweet above all that is sweet, and which is white above all that is white, yea, and pure above all that is pure" (Alma 32:42). We truly believed that our relationships could become so rewarding and satisfying that we would "feast upon this fruit even until [we were] filled, that [we would] hunger not, neither . . . thirst" (Alma 32:42), and we resolved to harvest the fruit with each other and our children.

Because Dave and I understood that these "sweet," "white," and "pure" experiences happened far too infrequently, we looked for specific instructions on nurturing our closest relationships. When we searched for the word *relationship* in the scriptures, we found passages about Zion-like societies that were of "one heart and one mind" (Moses 7:18) and the commandment to be "one" with each other and with Heavenly

Father and His Son: "That they all may be one; as thou, Father, art in me, and I in thee, that they also may be one in us" (John 17:21; see also D&C 38:27).

Through our further research on being one, we learned several important truths. First, we discovered that the Father and the Son are one not just because they possess the same powers, characteristics, and attributes but also because "the words and acts of one are the words and acts of the other." Accordingly, having faith in Heavenly Father is having faith in His Son.[2]

We learned that in order to become one with Them, we must strive "to do what Christ did and thus become like the Father": "Elohim is our God and he is Christ's God. The Son worships the Father, as we are commanded to do; if there is any being with whom we should feel a special kinship, it is with the Father. But Christ as the Only Begotten in the flesh, as the Redeemer, as the Savior, has made salvation possible and has become one with the Father. Thus salvation is in Christ; faith centers in him; and faithful saints have power to become like him and be as he is, even as he is as his Father."[3]

In other words, our interaction with the Father is through worship and prayer, in the name of His Son, and through the power of the Holy Ghost; but our relationship with the Son is a covenant relationship. Through the Savior's great "at-one-ment" and through our repentance and righteous works, we— who have been estranged from God through our sins and transgressions—can again become reconciled to, or set "at one" with, God.[4] As we follow the Savior in keeping baptismal and temple covenants, we become like Him—that is, we become "one" with Him and His Father. And the more we become one with Them, the more we are enabled to become one with each other. While striving to keep the commandments, our hearts are turned to love and serve our family members, and we are blessed with specific guidance to nourish those relationships. Thus, anything that enhances our covenant relationship with the Savior will also improve our relationships with each other.

In putting all these pieces together, we concluded that Heavenly Father's choicest blessings come to us as we strengthen our closest relationships. Notwithstanding our past failings, we realized that no sacrifice is too great to develop sweet, pure relationships with our family members. In addition to our patience, forgiveness, acceptance, encouragement, loyalty, and love, each opportunity to be with and serve one another would not be wasted—*if* the underlying emphasis were on preserving and strengthening these relationships.

After years of learning these great truths, our family sat down to watch Devin's video, something our children hadn't seen for a long time. Afterward, our older children were deeply upset that Devin "had to die." Dave and I tried to console them, saying the usual things: "He's waiting for us," "He's already made it to the celestial kingdom," and "We all want to be with him, so we need to follow Jesus."

In my heart, however, I felt their same sorrow, wishing that Devin could have been on earth to show them the ropes. How I longed for *all* of our children the experiences of growing up together and of building memories as a family. In this wistful moment of reflection, I was inspired to know that not only was Devin an unseen participant in our special family experiences on earth but, more important, someday, somehow, we would be endowed with a relationship with him—all without his physical presence on earth. Indeed, that same wonderful "sweet above all that which was sweet, white above all that is white, and pure above all that is pure" kind of familial relationship would be assured with our Devin.

In my previous reading of the Proclamation on the Family that "the divine plan of happiness enables family relationships to be perpetuated beyond the grave,"[5] I had assumed it referred to relationships that were already established, not ones that had little time to develop in mortality. But now I knew that creating memories and being with Devin on earth for a certain amount of time was not as important as our progress in this lifetime. Certainly, turning our hearts to each other here would guarantee us a special relationship with Devin there.

While trying to share this insight with our children, I

realized that *I* could not have understood its truth so many years before. It had taken a long time for me to appreciate the great importance of eternal relationships, of being one with Heavenly Father and His Son, as well as being one with each other.

As I allowed the significance of this prompting to sink in, I realized again that the spirit of Elijah had turned my heart—this time to my children on both sides of the veil. I recognized that the promise of being welded eternally to each of them was not just an ideal. Gaining "sweet," "white," and "pure" relationships truly is possible through obedience to the Savior and through acting upon powerful yearnings to nourish our eternal relationships with one another.

Chapter 15

THANK THE LORD THY GOD IN ALL THINGS

*D*ave and I did what we could to help our children appreciate their older brother, Devin. We took them with us to the hospital each year on his birthday, we showed them his scrapbook, we took pictures by "Devin's tree," and, whenever possible, we discussed his short life and any connecting gospel theme. Over time, we learned that keeping Devin's memory alive became an important means of recognizing the goodness of God in our lives.

We gratefully and willingly opened our hearts to Devin, even though we knew this could spark unexpected periods of longing and grieving. These waves of sorrow measured far less in intensity and frequency than we had known in the beginning, but their resulting pain still seemed to drown us with the same sense of vulnerability and defeat we had endured in the past.

When Devin had been gone eight years, we experienced a series of these setbacks during the anniversary of Devin's death. To begin with, I met and mourned with a young mother whose unborn child had developed a serious heart defect. Because her loss was so much like mine, observing her progress through pregnancy evoked many heartbreaking memories for me. Her sweet son, Ray, survived this life for only twenty-four hours; and at his graveside funeral, I silently reminisced about our own suffering as we had surrounded Devin's grave so long before.

Weeks later, with guarded emotions, we anticipated the day that Devin would have been baptized had he been alive. This day coincided with the day of our nephew's baptism. Because Brian's parents had thoughtfully asked us to participate in the meeting, I assumed supporting them would remove our sadness. But as I caught a glimpse of the tears rolling down the face of Brian's mother, I felt a familiar tug at my heart. How I longed to witness my own son's baptism and to experience those same tender feelings. I wasn't jealous or bitter, because I was truly happy for Brian and for his parents. I simply yearned for Devin and grieved for lost time and the earthly accomplishments he might have made.

Somewhere in my heartache that day, I was prompted to know that our second son, Michael, had been sent to us that we might experience the joy of raising a son who would be baptized, receive the priesthood, and serve a mission. This impression gave us an overwhelming gratitude for a sweet boy who raced to hug his parents for no apparent reason, who loved to kiss us on both cheeks every night, and who, like his sisters, "is part of the joy that helps us appreciate and put in perspective the sorrow that we experienced with Devin," as Dave wrote to a friend.

Days after Brian's baptism, our little family visited Devin's grave for Memorial Day. While cleaning his headstone and taking pictures, Dave and I noticed a young couple momentarily stop and hug at a small plot not far from us. We were saddened—but not surprised—to discover later that the grave belonged to a young child.

After returning home that day, I read a newspaper article summarizing the thoughts of parents who had lost children: "There are words for other people who lose loved ones— widows, widowers, orphans—but there is no word for a parent who loses a child, because it's a loss that is too awful to name." Another woman also lamented the loss of her son: "'I wish her all the happiness in the world,' said one mother about the woman who is her son's widow. 'But it's so easy for her. She can get a new husband . . . I can't get a new son.'"[1]

Almost shocked at these comments, I could not identify with such strong sentiments. Even though this season had brought more reminders of our loss than previous years, we could not deny the divine healing and sweet memories we had been given. We felt no resentment like that which we had read about in the paper, and we almost always took comfort in thinking about Devin.

As we evaluated our grief over eight years, we knew that because of the restored gospel, we were okay. Without the gospel, we would always have questioned Devin's short life, his suffering, and even his continued existence. With it, we could appreciate the comfort and guidance of the Holy Ghost and the recurring effects of the Atonement's healing.

Our healing truly had been a process, a sometimes rocky and haphazard two-steps-forward, one-step-back kind of chaos that could be plotted on a graph or a time line. By analyzing our development this way, we could compute the difference between where we had started and where we had come. Without doubt, we had come a long way.

But perhaps describing our up-and-down progress with statistics or trends didn't explain the inner, line-upon-line, continuous pattern underlying our experience of grief and divine healing. Applying an analogy we had grown to love, Dave and I realized that the Gardener of our flowerbeds consistently had pulled out the weeds of our lives and replaced them with wonderful, colorful flowers.[2]

Looking at our progress this way, we understood—and were thankful—that we weren't constantly struggling. The weeds of affliction were being removed, and flowers of peace, happiness, contentment, and spiritual growth were blooming in their place. While acknowledging the developing beauty of our garden, we further recognized that future weeds could also be removed with the help of the Lord.

Two years later, without setbacks or heartache, our gratitude deepened and blossomed again during the anniversaries of Devin's birth and death. As before, we celebrated Devin's birthday by delivering a gift to the hospital where Devin had spent his life. Inside, we showed our children the surgical washbasin where we had scrubbed our hands with small, soapy sponges, and we let them practice turning the water on and off with their knees. We were allowed to take our older children into the newborn intensive care unit to see where Devin had lived, and then we led all five of them into the hospice room where he had died. There, we reverently described the events that occurred on the day of Devin's death.

Driving home from the hospital, we opened Devin's scrapbook and read the letter Dave had written to Devin's future brothers and sisters. Not only did this letter evoke vivid memories of how hard it had been to let him go but it confirmed to our children our deep love for Devin and reminded us of the sweet, peaceful reassurance that we had done the right thing in submitting to the will of the Lord.

The following day, we gathered with extended family members and ate angel food cake in remembrance of Devin's birthday and chocolate cake to celebrate the birthday of our nephew, Brian. Thankfully, we rejoiced in his growth, recognizing that we were not resentful that Devin was not experiencing similar progress.

With the same group, Dave later shared his reflections of our sacred and sweet experiences with Devin. He said he could still picture the beautiful summer day when he had stood under the shade of a large tree to pay tribute to "our brave little boy." Dave remembered his feelings of respect for life, reverence for death, and gratitude to Heavenly Father for knowing Devin could be eternally ours. Dave explained that our experience had changed his entire outlook on what was important in life—it had motivated him to love our children more fully and to develop strong relationships with them. Because of this, Dave concluded that he would forever be grateful that Devin had passed through his life.

To honor Devin one more time, we again drove to the cemetery with our children to celebrate Devin's "Heaven Day," the anniversary of his death and return to heaven. This time, I took doughnuts as a treat and we saluted Devin with a "halo toast" while sitting around his grave. We then wandered through the rest of the cemetery, occasionally stopping to notice a particular headstone on the way. All of our children sensed the reverence of the day. Our five-year-old son went from grave to grave, tracing his fingers in the grooves of the names on the headstones; our seven-year-old daughter took note of all the pretty silk flowers, pinwheels, and flags and asked to place similar items at Devin's grave.

As the evening drew to a close, we gratefully acknowledged the grace of the Lord in our lives—for after ten years, the holidays and the anniversaries of Devin's birth and death had become sweet, peaceful, and unifying. Sharing Devin's life and death with our children had become very important to us, and we understood that as they knew and loved Devin, they would strive to follow the dictates of the Holy Ghost and be enabled to return to live with him again.

These wonderful experiences taught us the importance and power of gratitude. Whether we had sorrowed in our setbacks or had rejoiced in our family unity, we had discovered that expressing gratitude to Heavenly Father shows "our dependence upon a higher source of wisdom and knowledge" and gives a "calming peace—a peace which allows us to not canker our souls for what we don't have . . . [and which] helps us overcome the pain of adversity and failure."[3]

As we "thank the Lord [our] God in all things" (D&C 59:7), we are grateful "for what happens, not only for the good things in life but also for the opposition and challenges of life that add to our experience and faith. We put our lives in His hands, realizing that all that transpires will be for our experience."[4] We therefore concluded we must thank Heavenly Father for the flowers *and* the weeds!

Understanding better the significance of our gratitude in all seasons, we found in the hymn "Come, Thou Fount of Every Blessing" the formula for showing gratitude. This song refers to the time when Samuel of old demonstrated his gratitude to the Lord by placing a stone on the ground of a specific battlefield. Samuel called the stone *Ebenezer,* meaning "stone of help." This memorial identified where the Lord had blessed them in their combat and was "a token of gratitude for deliverance from the Philistines."[5]

We, too, must "raise [our] Ebenezer" to show gratitude for deliverance from our afflictions. Our token of gratitude must start by acknowledging the Savior as the "fount," or the source, of every blessing, that "hither by [His] help I come." Truly, we must "tune [our] heart[s]" and sing praises for "His precious blood," the blood that rescues us from danger and takes us back to the "fold of God."[6]

Moreover, because we are "prone to wander" when we forget the ever-constant blessings of the Atonement, we must "live in thanksgiving daily" (Alma 34:38). We must express daily gratitude to Heavenly Father, and we must continually follow His Son, because "obedience to the laws, ordinances, and commandments is the greatest expression of love and gratitude that we can bestow upon [the Lord]."[7]

Our humble gratitude will be shown as we testify "with the voice of thanksgiving, and tell of all thy wondrous works" (Psalm 26:7), especially the blessings we had been given from our challenging and extraordinary experiences on earth. Our continual care to do so will cause us to plead again and again,

> *Here's my heart, Lord,*
> *Take and seal it*
> *Seal it for Thy courts above.*[8]

Through His infinite grace, the Savior can then bind our wandering hearts to Him.

Chapter 16

Faith, Hope, and Charity

A decade without Devin also marked a decade of growth for our little family. One Christmas, I decided to write children's books to capture the diverse personalities of each of our children, including Devin. Though I had never attempted such an undertaking, creating these stories generated another unexpected journey of discovery from our experiences with Devin.

The first five books were fun and light-hearted, but Devin's book carried a more thoughtful tone and summarized our experience of losing of a loved one. Entitled *The Little Boy with a Broken Heart,* the story is really about the little boy's parents, who are mourning his death. In their sadness, they cannot see the special gift their son has given them, even though they think about him constantly and do many things to remember him.

After a long time passes, the parents become less and less sad. They begin to enjoy the beauty of spring flowers and autumn leaves again, and each day, the gift from the little boy with a broken heart seems a little closer and a little clearer.

On a very ordinary day, the mother and father somehow feel and understand the special gift, even though it has been with them all along. They see his gift in the laughter of children and in the changes of a beautiful sunset, and his gift makes all their sadness meaningful and bearable. They discover that the gift from the little boy with a broken heart is an appreciation for life and a beacon of hope for a bright future.

Composing this little story was a marvelously rewarding process, for it helped us to define the hope that Dave and I had gained from our experience with Devin, it motivated us to remember him, and it was a tangible way to share his life with others, especially with our own children.

This story inspired me to think about Ryan's Lion and the similar lions we had sent to others. I now wondered how a stuffed animal had given us such comfort. It certainly wasn't magical or powerful, and it really couldn't give courage to anyone. It wasn't even alive!

After discussing this question, Dave and I concluded that Ryan's Lion represented a fellowship with others who were suffering. Precisely because it had been a gift from those who had struggled with their afflictions and eventually overcame them, we had been given hope to endure our own. And as we had passed on Ryan's Lion, we had felt a sense of healing, knowing others would be given courage to brave their challenges, as well.

This answer was added upon one morning when I awoke with the words of Moroni echoing in my mind: "And charity suffereth long, and is kind, and envieth not, and is not puffed up, seeketh not her own, is not easily provoked, thinketh no evil, and rejoiceth not in iniquity but rejoiceth in the truth, beareth all things, believeth all things, hopeth all things, endureth all things" (Moroni 7:45).

Ryan's Lion not only represents courage and fellowship but also symbolizes the pure, enduring love of Jesus Christ. Now understanding the connection between a stuffed animal and charity, I wrote *The Story of Ryan's Lion*. At the beginning of this tale, a tiny baby boy named Ryan is born several weeks early and needs special doctors to fix his small heart. Worried that Ryan will need courage when he must stay in the hospital alone, his parents find a little stuffed lion and call it Ryan's Lion. When Ryan gets better, he gives his lion to a father and mother who need strength while their son awaits a heart transplant.

From there, Ryan's Lion is given to a young woman serving as a missionary for her church, to a family whose sister is born with a serious birth defect, to a couple whose baby suddenly becomes very ill and dies, to a young girl whose family won't support her religious beliefs, to a grandfather dying in the hospital, and to a young woman struggling with her testimony and self-worth.

Every person who holds Ryan's Lion becomes a little braver, a bit more giving, and a littler stronger inside. And each person gradually learns that part of the magic of a ragged, stuffed lion is found in passing it on.

The story ends with baby Ryan having grown to be a ten-year-old boy with a big heart. He sometimes talks about his surgery and reveals the long scar on his chest. But the real story of Ryan's Lion never ends, for it continues to give courage to all who hold it, feel its strength, and give it to others.

In the course of writing this story, I realized that as healing means seeking the Savior's love and allowing Him to weed and cultivate our mortal gardens, charity means sharing that courage and hope from Him with others. Thus, the message of Ryan's Lion is charity: find the Savior's strength and pass it on.

Once I realized the importance of hope and charity in our healing process, I was determined to know how faith had guided us in our time of grief. Through weeks of research, I was directed to learn about developing childlike faith. I first read that I would remain a "natural man" and "an enemy to God," unless I yielded "to the enticings of the Holy Spirit, . . . and becometh as a child, submissive, meek, humble, patient, full of love, willing to submit to all things which the Lord seeth fit to inflict upon him, even as a child doth submit to his father" (Mosiah 3:19).

Then I found that the Savior commanded his disciples to "be converted, and become as little children" (Matthew 18:1–5), meaning, as Elder James E. Talmage said: "Christ would not have had His chosen representatives become childish. . . . He would have them become childlike . . . in obedience, truthfulness, trustfulness, purity, humility, and faith."[1]

While letting the distinction between "childish" and "childlike" sink in, I remembered meeting a young girl with this pure childlike faith. She had made such an impression on me that Dave and I named our first daughter after her. With this experience in mind, I began writing the concluding story of my trilogy, *More like Lauren.*

This story describes six-year old Lauren as a beautiful girl with strawberry blonde hair and a bright smile. Lauren is full of sunshine, and through many experiences, she demonstrates her childlike nature of being gentle and patient, obedient and teachable, prayerful, believing and trustful, and full of love. And because of her example, those around her want to become "more like Lauren."

The plot unfolds as Lauren meets a young woman who is grieving for the loss of her son. Deciding to cheer her up, Lauren tells all about her brother, Cameron, and happily explains how she was born with Cameron's tint of red hair and how Cameron died while sleeping in his crib.

Because the young woman is so heartbroken, she simply listens. But Lauren's innocence and trusting nature are not forgotten as the woman later works to acquire more childlike faith, like Lauren's. She resolves to become more loving by helping others in need; to become more believing by trusting that she will be with her son again; to become more prayerful by asking for courage, wisdom, and peace; to become obedient and teachable in learning from her disappointment and sadness; and to become gentle and patient with herself and with those who don't understand her situation. Someday, she will feel the sunshine return to her life as she becomes more like Lauren.

Satisfied with the results of this story, I sincerely appreciated my own need to develop childlike faith. I discussed it with Dave, prayed about it, and pondered its meaning in the temple. There I realized for the first time the childlike faith of Adam and Eve, not only in their innocence in the Garden of Eden but also in their lone and dreary world as they continued to exercise submissive, humble, and prayerful faith.

Like them, I had been taught in safe havens and had been given opportunities to exercise faith in an atmosphere of peace and security. When Devin died, I left that state of innocence, and now I humbly recognized that, unlike Adam and Eve, I had not always applied or cultivated the faith I had been taught in my childhood Garden.

Dave and I further recognized that the only way we can become "spiritually begotten," or "children of Christ, his sons, and his daughters" (Mosiah 5:7), is by exercising continual childlike faith—in our gardens of innocence *and* in our times of tribulation. Surely, we must not allow our experiences and limited knowledge to interfere with our ability to exercise child-like faith and thus receive the daily blessings of the Atonement.

When these three stories were completed, Dave and I acknowledged with gratitude that our entire experience with Devin—bringing him into the world, submitting to the will of the Father in letting him go, grieving his loss, enduring our sorrow, and mourning with others—was all about faith, hope, and charity.

Once we discovered how these virtues had carried us in our past afflictions, we couldn't help but notice how faith, hope, and charity could guide us in our present circumstances and could focus our efforts in the future.

Chapter 17

A NEW STANDARD IS SET

Dave and I seemed to find faith, hope, and charity together every time we opened the scriptures, read from the words of the prophets, and sang from the hymn-book. Over time, these three virtues provided a new basis of gospel understanding and set a new standard for developing our own faith, hope, and charity.

While witnessing the unwavering conviction of close friends, we were taught poignantly about the principle of faith. One friend lost both her husband and their newborn in a terrible automobile accident. Her husband had been the light and love of her life, and we wondered how she could bear to lose her confidant, companion, and provider—as well as her sweet infant son.

Another couple suddenly lost their fourth child from the same medical condition that had taken their first baby. While this was hard enough, they learned that the same tragedy might result if they brought more children into the world.

We felt we could not have survived such tremendous losses, and like our own past heartache, their current sorrows did not carry a guaranteed timetable for healing. For the first time in many years, I questioned how such terrible things could happen to good, faithful people, especially those who had already been through the refiner's fire.

Their ongoing afflictions seemed as unfair and relentless as the continual struggles of others we knew: my sister, whose entire world had been rearranged by multiple sclerosis; a friend whose husband had forsaken his spiritual beliefs; and a young woman who continually had been drawn into abusive relationships.

Despite carrying such heavy burdens, however, each of these individuals remained obedient and trusting. Our friend who had lost her husband and baby invited a struggling young woman to live with her and subsequently influenced her decision to serve a mission. The couple who lost two infant children continued to serve in Church leadership positions, inspiring others with their enduring dedication to each other and to the Lord.

Likewise, my sister confronted her health problems with spiritual ammunition. She resolved to live life to its fullest by focusing on her family and other important relationships. The woman whose husband had left the Church resumed the responsibility of teaching their children the importance of the gospel and the sacrifice of the Savior. And despite her uphill climb, our friend who had endured several abusive relationships persisted in seeking for and following the promptings of the Spirit. She became determined to stop the chain of abuse and to understand her eternal worth through earnest prayers, scripture study, and temple attendance.

Witnessing such faith reminded us "that sometimes the Savior calms the storm. Sometimes He lets the storm rage and calms you."[1] Though the furious tempests still encircled our dear friends, each of them had resolved to stay in the boat with the Savior, for "No waters can swallow the ship where lies / The Master of ocean and earth and skies" (*Hymns,* 1985, no. 105). Indeed, they would not be alone to weather the storm, and He would steer them safely Home.

This underlying trust was also exhibited by Shadrach, Meshach, and Abed-nego. Knowing their God *could* deliver them, these disciples of old yet concluded, "But if not," which simply meant but if He *doesn't* deliver us, "we will not serve thy gods, nor worship the golden image which thou has set up" (Daniel 3:17–18).

Elder Dennis E. Simmons taught that exercising this same kind of "but-if-not" faith is the way we should approach our earthly trials: "Our God will deliver us from ridicule and persecution, *but if not. . . .* Our God will deliver us from sickness and disease, *but if not. . . .* He will deliver us from loneliness, depression, or fear, *but if not. . . .* Our God will deliver us from threats, accusations, and insecurity, *but if not. . . .* He will deliver us from death or impairment of loved ones, *but if not . . . we will trust in the Lord.*[2]

Though we acknowledged our faith to be nowhere near this level, Dave and I also recognized this as the type of faith we should strive to develop.

Appreciating this new standard, in turn, caused us to seek a better yardstick for measuring our hope. Dave and I read of a young woman who had testified of her belief in the gospel and in Christ but who doubted she personally was "capable and worthy of achieving eternal life." Her stake president admonished that if she really believed the Lord could save her, she also should believe in her "capacity to take advantage of his atonement." We, too, must have faith and hope in the Lord *and* in ourselves, looking "beyond weaknesses, sins, and fears, believing that all is possible through the atonement of Jesus Christ, and that our honest efforts will bear fruit."[3]

This woman came to appreciate that hope is more than wishful thinking; it is an "expectation" of things to come, or "the confident expectation of and longing for the promised blessings of righteousness . . . [and the] anticipation of eternal life through faith in Jesus Christ."[4]

Thus, we should *expect* the Lord to keep His promises of eternal life with our loved ones, and we should *expect* ourselves to gain those promises through the grace of the Savior and through our obedience to His commandments and the whisperings of the Spirit.

Furthermore, we found that this kind of hope is purposely interrelated with our faith. Hope can motivate us to exercise the "but-if-not" kind of faith, for "power to do anything with the help of the Lord quite literally depends upon the degree to which we are willing to hope for, and to expect, that help."[5]

For example, we have faith that God exists and loves us, and we have hope in the promise that He will hear and answer our prayers. Because of this faith and hope, we trust Him and seek Him through sincere prayer and scripture reading. Likewise, we have faith that the Savior's Atonement was wrought to help us with all of life's experiences, and we have hope that we can be forgiven of our sins, strengthened during our earthly trials, and healed from our suffering. Thus, we humbly repent of our wrongdoings and come unto the Savior through obedience.

These attempts to remain committed to the gospel further reinforce our faith and hope, deepening our trust in the Savior, brightening our expectation of the future, and ultimately leading us to the pure love of Christ.

But like faith and hope, true charity is something bestowed

upon us from the Lord, and it involves much more than we had previously learned. Charity is not just serving others, strengthening relationships, and mourning with those that mourn. Specifically, "forgiveness, in its fullest expression, is synonymous with charity, the pure love of Christ." Forgiveness "is a personal attribute, not just a decision we make from time to time when we feel we should." Because those with a forgiving heart "see the world in a different light," they "forsake the tendency to judge, condemn, exclude, or hate any human soul," they seek "to love and to be patient with imperfection," and they recognize "that all are in need of the atonement of Jesus Christ."[6]

This deeper understanding caused me to realize a need to forgive those who had not understood my intense sorrow years before. At a very critical time of mourning, I had been deeply hurt when several individuals indicated that I should overlook Devin's anniversaries and birthdays. Assuming they had not wanted me to remember or honor Devin, I tried to defend my way of grieving and later determined to avoid them and this kind of contention again.

While I was looking back to this experience, a good friend helped me realize for the first time that because *their* way of grieving included avoiding certain situations and emotions, these individuals had wanted me to escape unnecessary suffering, as well. Out of love for me, they truly had wanted to "take away my pain," or at least insulate me from the full extent of my sorrow.

This insight changed how I viewed the entire situation and my subsequent hard feelings. I didn't regret my past way of grieving—I was grateful to have remembered Devin and to have felt the associated pain. But now, knowing the intent of their hearts, I was given a more Christlike love for them and enabled to forgive them for the heartache they had unintentionally caused.

With this heavy burden lifted, I learned for myself that of faith, hope, charity, "the greatest of these is charity" (1 Corinthians 13:13). It is the greatest because it is the love that Christ has for all of us. But perhaps charity is also the greatest because it is the most difficult of the three to acquire through our faithfulness. Charity incorporates faith and hope as it involves interaction with and love for others. In other words, I could personally increase my hope and faith through prayer, scripture study, and obedience; but, without reaching out to others, I could never be given this all-encompassing acceptance, regard, and love for mankind.

The resulting culmination of our research was the gradual witness that faith, hope, and charity are more than just great virtues we ought to possess—they are essential for becoming like the Savior and being "saved in the kingdom of God" (Moroni 10:20–21). Along with "feasting upon the word of

Christ and enduring to the end," faith, hope, and charity are truly "the way" we "shall have eternal life": "Ye must press forward with a steadfastness in Christ [faith], having a perfect brightness of hope, and a love of God and of all men [charity]" (2 Nephi 31:19–21).

With these new standards, we had a deepened resolve to exercise childlike *and* "but-if-not" faith, to have hope in the future *and* to have an expectation for the promises of the Savior, and to reach out to those in need *and* to seek a forgiving and charitable heart. Now we just needed the knowledge and wisdom to strive for them.

Chapter 18

A LIFETIME OF TUTORIALS

O ur desire to become more faithful, hopeful, and charitable increased our humility. Dave and I recognized
the Lord's healing hand in our lives as we envisioned
the long road of work ahead of us. At times, we wondered if we
would live long enough to develop and to be given the qualities of faith, hope, and charity.

To understand our ultimate potential, we first reflected
upon our past progress. We realized that as we had cycled again
and again through the grieving process, we had struggled back
and forth on a continuum of opposites: faith, hope, and charity on one side and doubt, despair, and selfishness on the other.

Our initial hope and faith had been based on eventual outcomes or certain conditions. In the beginning, our faith and
hope had centered on our desire for Devin to be sealed to us,
for his name to be placed on a transplant list, and for him to

receive a heart transplant. In the depths of our grief, our faith and hope had been focused on being healed on our own terms, instead of upon the Lord's timetable.

When some of these unrealistic or unlikely expectations had not been achieved, doubt and despair replaced our hope and faith. This doubt had surfaced many times when I had questioned the breadth and depth of the Atonement or my testimony of the gospel. Despair had been evidenced by the depression I had endured while discovering suffering all around me.

Possibly as a result of such doubt and despair, selfishness then had manifested itself while I was in "survival mode," when my focus had been mostly self-centered. I remembered withholding my support from others, turning away from relationships, and being self-absorbed in my sorrow. Though I couldn't have done any better at the time, I now understood that this had been the adversary's continual pull toward the wrong end of the continuum.

As the years had passed, our doubt, despair, and selfishness fluctuated, declining only as we had learned more about the gospel, the Savior, faith, hope, and charity. Our faith and hope had been strengthened when our overwhelming grief drove us to learn more about Heavenly Father and His plan of salvation and when our deep humility had compelled us to appreciate our covenant relationship with the Savior and the necessity of relying solely upon His merits to heal us.

Our charity also had changed noticeably since the early days of selfishness and self-absorption. Our reaching out to others evolved from merely validating others' suffering to emphasizing the great importance of turning to the Savior. We had gained a type of compassion that leads to a charitable heart—but we also knew that developing even tiny seeds of charity was not something we had done, or could have done, on our own.

After more than a decade, we gratefully acknowledged the gift from the Savior: we had been given line upon line, grace upon grace, until our hearts had been purged at least somewhat of the weeds of disbelief, despair, and selfishness, and we had been sanctified with small but brilliant flowers of faith, hope, and charity.

Moreover, recognizing these blessings gave us hope to build upon our progress in the future. We learned from Sister Patricia T. Holland, who expressed that she is "convinced of, and thrilled by, the thought that God has a will, a plan for me personally" and that "God made each of us for an individually tailored and divine purpose. We each have a divine errand, and therein lies our joy."[1]

Each of our customized plans includes specific person-alities, strengths, weaknesses, and spiritual gifts, as well as individualized tutorials that provide us with experience, wisdom, understanding, and compassion. Though some of our tutorials may simply be Church callings, friendships with certain people, participation in temple ordinances, educational and vocational pursuits, missionary service, repentance, scriptural inquiries, and parenting experiences, others come in the form of trials and obstacles.

Elder Neal A. Maxwell explained that "the most advanced disciples—far from being immune from further instruction— experience even deeper and more constant tutorials." These divine tutorials are "given especially to [the Savior's] friends— those who believe in and who strive to follow Him." They are "enriching, but stretching" and can sanctify and purify us for future exaltation.[2]

When my maternal grandmother passed away, Dave and I realized that she had submitted to a lifetime of tutorials, including many divine tutorials. They had enabled the transformation of her very nature to seasoned faith, hope, and charity. Despite losing her husband and enduring countless health problems, her faith in the Savior and her hope for the future had only increased throughout the years.

Grandma had consciously cultivated the art of charity. After she died, we learned that she had spent the days following her husband's death delivering the flowers from his funeral to her friends in rest homes. This act of kindness was an effort to keep from feeling sorry for herself, even at a time when she had every right to. Because of Grandma's great love for others, people were always drawn to her and a measure of this same charity had returned to her. She was radiant, happy, and joyful until the day she died, for "whoso is found possessed of [charity] at the last day, it shall be well with him" (Moroni 7:47).

Dave and I observed that all four of our grandmothers had developed very different lives of faith, hope, and charity. Each of them had attended Devin's graveside services, each of them had "died in faith" (Hebrews 11:13), and each of them had lived long enough to obtain the pure love of Christ. Maybe they specifically had prayed "unto the Father with all the energy of heart, that [they] may be filled with this love, which he hath bestowed upon all who are true followers of his Son" (Moroni 7:48). Yet, all of our grandmothers followed their own path with humility and meekness (Moroni 7:43–44) and profited from a lifetime of experiences and divine tutorials. Their faith, hope, and charity increased and ultimately culminated in their each becoming like the Savior.

As we spoke of one of our favorite quotations, Dave and I realized again that our Heavenly Father certainly would not deny any of His spirit children the opportunity to develop these divine qualities throughout mortality: "No pain that we suffer, no trial that we experience is wasted. It ministers to our education to the development of such qualities as patience, faith, fortitude and humility. All that we suffer, all that we endure, especially when we endure it patiently, builds up our character, purifies our hearts, expands our souls and makes us more tender and charitable."[3]

Initially, we had been drawn to this message because it had answered the question of why mankind must suffer. But over time we learned that "all things are given them which are expedient unto man" (2 Nephi 2:27; see also vv. 26, 28–29). In other words, Heavenly Father will bestow upon us all the necessary opportunities and experiences to move us away from doubt, despair, and selfishness and to bring us closer toward the Christlike attributes of faith, hope, and charity.

Thus, we could anticipate that our personal plans would contain *many* tutorials to guide us in becoming more like the Savior—just as our grandmothers had been guided. Likewise, we also could expect that after doing "all we can do" (2 Nephi 25:23) in choosing "liberty and eternal life through the great Mediator" (2 Nephi 2:27), His grace would save us and help us to become like Him.

Our divine tutorial of losing Devin was the catalyst for learning and embracing these and other gospel truths. While the passage of time and working through our grief had brought about a certain resolution to our mourning, only our understanding and internalizing of truth could provide us with real healing—the Savior's healing. Through our reception of the

Lord's Atonement, the experience of having and then losing Devin unclouded the veil between this life and the next so that the whole plan of salvation became simple and perfect, making every other system defective in comparison. And, quite possibly, no other event in our lives could have provided us with such a clear and lasting perspective or appreciation for the comprehensive healing of the Savior.

Chapter 19

JOY COMETH IN
THE MORNING

*C*lear and lasting perspective and comprehensive healing
could very well define what joy in the morning means
after weeping throughout the long night (Psalm 30:5).
We felt true joy mixed with heartache on many occasions, but
the long night of grief and gradual healing blessed us with a joy
that could not be compared to anything we previously had
experienced.

Had we not been required to leave our own Garden of
Eden, we would have "remained in a state of innocence, having no joy, for [we] knew no misery" (2 Nephi 2:23). Through
"opposition in all things" (2 Nephi 2:11; see also vv. 22–23),
we could now appreciate that joy will come in the morning of
the resurrection *and* that joy can come in the morning of our
mortal afflictions (2 Nephi 2:25; see also Moses 5:10).

Recognizing the fruits of joy from our experience with

Devin was a humbling, exhilarating process. One such discovery was made while learning about "comfort in the hour of death" from the teachings of President Heber J. Grant:

"To a Latter-day Saint, while death brings sorrow into our homes and our hearts, that sorrow is more or less of the same nature that we feel when we are temporarily called upon to part with our dear ones who are going out into the mission field or who are moving away for some time. That awful anguish that I have seen exhibited by those who know not the truth, I believe never comes into the heart of a true Latter-day Saint."[1]

Though at first I wondered how someone so well acquainted with death could dismiss the agonizing grief of others so easily, I was taught the significance of this statement after a friend described the unbearable suspense of waiting for her oldest son to return from the mission field. Her missionary's flight home was scheduled that week, and she excitedly told me all about the preparations being made to his old room, the anticipated plans at the airport, and the scheduled family celebration to be held in their home.

A week later, my friend was glowing with an irrepressible smile and a light in her eyes. Without waiting to be asked, she detailed the first moments of seeing her son step off the airplane and her feelings of happiness and gratitude while hearing his missionary experiences and testimony the following Sunday.

Her joy was full—the arrival of her son was almost too good to be true.

With this experience in the back of my mind, I told our daughter Anna that Devin (her four-year-old friend) would be playing at our house. She exclaimed in a silly voice, "You mean *my brother,* Devin?!?" Not expecting to hear her say that, my heart skipped a beat, thinking how wonderful it would be to have *our* Devin return home.

For the next couple days, I repeatedly got that Christmas Eve kind of excitement that something spectacular was going to happen. Eventually, I realized I was thinking about a homecoming for our Devin. It wouldn't be anytime soon, but I knew our reunion with Devin would be just as marvelous, if not more so, as when a child returns home from the mission field.

When I relayed this impression to Dave, we were both interested that I hadn't felt even a twinge of sadness while thinking about seeing Devin again. On the contrary, it was thrilling to gain this glimpse of heaven, understanding what our reunion with him will be like.

Months after this experience, we rejoiced as we read three journal entries that demonstrated that our children were also benefiting from Devin's life and death. The first entry described going to the cemetery one spring day to plant flowers at Devin's grave. After pushing the dirt around the base of the pansies, our six-year-old son, Michael, carefully explained to his younger sisters Elizabeth and Claire that Devin's body would rejoin his spirit upon his resurrection. Unlike in the past, we had not prompted this discussion, but it was apparent that our children's knowledge of the Resurrection was more than an abstract concept. It had become so connected with Devin that our children had no doubts that Jesus had been resurrected or that they would see their older brother again.

Another account from my journal detailed the events of the night our children had said their final good-byes to their great-grandmother. Although she was in a coma, Dave's maternal grandma had briefly opened her eyes, acknowledging our presence as we had entered her hospital room. At first, our children had been reluctant to say anything, but within a few minutes they each took a turn holding Grandma's hand and telling her how much they loved her. When all became quiet, we offered a prayer and sang a Primary song together.

Our older daughters had realized Grandma's nearness to the veil of death. Without telling anyone, eight-year-old Abby slipped behind a curtain, knelt beside an empty hospital bed, and prayed that Grandma might have a chance to meet Devin after she died. About the same time, ten-year-old Lauren rested her head on Grandma's shoulder; and, with tears in her eyes, whispered to Grandma how much we would miss her. In amazement, Dave and I exchanged glances, grateful that our children sensed the significance of such a tender moment.

The last entry related the experience of delivering colorful balloons to a small grave near our home. Each helium balloon contained a personalized message to celebrate the first birthday of a close friend's baby—a sweet girl named Chloe who had died before our daughter Emma was born. One balloon read, "Happy Birthday, Chloe. I love you and I like you." Another said, "Hope you have a great birthday. Write back soon."

While one of our young daughters had not wanted to send her yellow balloon heavenward to Chloe, the rest of us had watched happily until all the other balloons were no longer in sight. Before we left the cemetery, one child picked up some pretty rocks and leaves to take back to Chloe's parents—all so that they could remember her better.

Dave and I realized that each of these accounts represented a sweet, powerful illustration that our children were developing their own faith, hope, and charity. Without intentionally teaching them these virtues, we perceived they also were learning about the importance of faith in the Savior and the plan of salvation, hope for a bright future with our family members, and charity to reach out to those in need. Though our children were still young, we recognized in some small degree that we "have no greater joy than to hear that [our] children walk in truth" (3 John 1:4).

Lastly, we experienced true joy as we renewed friendships with nearly a dozen friends who had suffered various losses of loved ones over the years. Not unpredictably, these friends also had discerned the healing hand of the Savior in their lives and had also felt the reassurance and peace of the gospel in a profound, transforming manner. Through "difficult blessings"—as one friend called the loss of his daughter—each of us had faced similar divine tutorials and experienced an enlarging of our hearts, a deepening of our spiritual senses, and an increased appreciation of life itself.

Rekindling these friendships was comparable to the reunion of Alma and the sons of Mosiah upon completion of their many years of missionary labors. Like us, they truly must have rejoiced that their brethren had endured well and had become increasingly faithful through "their sufferings in the land, their sorrows, and their afflictions, and their incomprehensible joy" (Alma 28:8; also 27:16–17).

Dave and I concluded that because of the Savior, we could "taste the bitter" of our sorrows *and* "know to prize the good" (Moses 6:55) of mortality. By turning our lives over to the Lord, we could remain vulnerable to our earthly challenges— not paralyzed by fear but confidently trusting our Heavenly Father and being "willing to submit to all things"(Mosiah 3:19).

Likewise, we could testify "the trial of [our] faith [had become] much more precious than of gold that perisheth" (1 Peter 1:7), for "our light affliction, which is but for a moment, worketh for us a far more exceeding and eternal weight of glory" (2 Corinthians 4:17).

The joy we had gained throughout our long night of mourning balanced all our heartache into a sweet harmony whose two parts were incomplete without the other. The lonely, melancholy tune of our sorrow, when blended with the sweet melody of the Savior's love, had become music to us—a song we were grateful to have sung, a song that would continue to carry the beautiful strains of unity, strength, and inspiration. Truly, joy had come in the morning.

*   *   *

Obviously, our lives continued after we had arrived at such an epiphany. Many times, I have found myself on the wrong side of the faith, hope, and charity continuum, falling prey to doubt, despair, and selfishness as I have read of wars and disasters around the world, as I have witnessed the adversary's brutal hold on dear friends, or as I have discovered the hazardous temptations our children face.

Even during one challenging pregnancy, I was discouraged to encounter doubtful, despairing, and selfish tendencies while bringing a child into the world—just as I had encountered when sending one into the next. With such amazing and enlightening experiences in our lives, I have often wondered how I ever could lose sight of the importance of faith, hope, and charity and the resulting feelings of joy.

Over the years, we have sensed that joy can be transient but it also can be found again and again. Friends who have lost loved ones have taught us that the secret to reacquiring joy lies in building upon the truths we have learned from our tutorials and realizing anew the healing of the Savior. And perhaps the best secret is to seek for joy—His joy—every morning.

PART 3

Some Suggestions for

Grieving and Healing

Chapter 20

LOOK TO GOD
AND LIVE AGAIN

*L*ike so many others, Elder Lance B. Wickman of the Seventy understands from a "poignant personal experience that there is no night quite so dark as the loss of a child." He has counseled bereaved parents to "first . . . know that grief is the natural by-product of love. One cannot selflessly love another person and not grieve at his suffering or eventual death."[1] Along with his words of wisdom, I offer the following suggestions for those who grieve and those who seek for healing.

FIND SOLACE IN YOUR MEMORIES

First of all, take comfort in knowing you did all you could do for your loved one, for "such faith, fasting, and blessing could not be in vain! That your child did not recover in spite of all that was done in his behalf can and should be the basis for peace and reassurance to all who love him! The Lord—who inspires the blessings and who hears every earnest prayer—called him home nonetheless. *All the experiences of prayer, fasting, and faith may well have been more for our benefit than for his.*"[2]

In addition, find solace in doing those things that can help you remember your loved one. While the memories are still fresh, compile and detail records of his or her life and include photographs, videos, and other significant keepsakes. Create meaningful traditions or experiences to bring closure or to preserve the memory of your loved one.

UNDERSTAND GRIEF ITSELF

To gain appropriate expectations of your reactions to your loss, it is helpful to understand the process of grieving, its various cycles, and its common reactions.[3] Recognize your responses and emotions as you experience them and strive to learn from your setbacks in the healing process.

Recognize that you and your spouse will grieve in very different ways: Your "ups and downs will not always coincide." "In reality, when a couple is grieving, neither can consistently have the emotional strength to fill the needs of the other."[4] Nevertheless, strive for open communication and patience with each other.

If you have other children, do your best to explain the death of their sibling in a simple and truthful manner. Young children "may not have enough words or the right words for their grief, and they may not know how to respond to the feelings they have. . . . They usually react through behavior—either acting out, withdrawing or repressing the painful events." Because you may be emotionally drained, invite a special teacher, counselor, or good friend to support your children in their grief. Do all you can to assure your children that you still love them and "accept their feelings as legitimate." Be prepared to answer their questions again and again.[5]

WORK THROUGH YOUR GRIEF

Accept that "healing hurts" and that "you must acknowledge and *feel* the hurt."[6] Spiritual feelings sometimes are blocked out until the pain is felt, and suppressed pain often manifests itself in some other form, such as physical ailments, anxiety, depression, and so forth. At the same time, however, balance working through your grief and resting from it. Replenish yourself with spiritual resources, exercise, sleep, and good nutrition.

Even though "much of the work of healing is done alone, inside the heart, in the company of the Spirit of the Lord," do not minimize "the marvelous power that comes from the help and compassion of others."[7] Teach others how to listen, and encourage them to pray and fast for you. Try to be patient and forgiving with those who do not understand your grief and recognize their efforts to comfort you, rather than dwelling on the exact words they have spoken. Respond to well-meaning but seemingly insensitive comments with your own feelings, saying something like "Thank you for thinking of us in our time of sorrow," or "I used to think that way, too, before I lost a child."

Ultimately, be patient with yourself, because "grief is not something that you can just shut off at the end of a given amount of time. We can only rebuild our lives if we allow ourselves the time we need to work through our loss . . . *time* to resolve those questions or feelings that can be resolved . . . and *time* to allow us to accept those questions that have no answers."[8]

SEEK THE SAVIOR'S HEALING

Understand the critical role of the Savior in your spiritual healing, and "walk away from the darkness and come into the light, his light, with meekness and lowliness of heart."[9]

"Healing is not only private, it is sacred. There is something so sacred about partaking of the power of the Atonement to overcome suffering, disappointment, or sin that it happens in the privacy of that special relationship between the mortal and the divine. Healing involves a private, personal communion with the Savior, the Master Healer."[10]

Maintain your faithful trust in Him. "Do not ever doubt the goodness of God, even if you do not know 'why.' . . . Mortality's supreme test is to face the 'why' and then let it go, trusting humbly in the Lord's promise that 'all things must come to pass in their time' (D&C 64:32)."[11]

As Elder Neal A. Maxwell counseled, rather "than pacing up and down within the cell of our circumstance," strive to endure well, "not merely [through] the passage of time, but the passage of the soul—and not merely from A to B, but sometimes all the way from A to Z."[12] This means qualifying for the strength of the Lord by following His commandments faithfully.

Specifically, heed the advice of Elder Henry B. Eyring throughout your trials: "The first, middle, and the last thing to do is to pray." Then "read and ponder the standard works of the Church and the words of living prophets"; "go to your meetings, even when it seems hard"; partake of the sacrament and renew your covenants in order to have His Spirit always; and accept any call to serve in the Lord's church, for "any call to serve in it is a call to serve Him."[13]

Continue to search for answers to your questions, and prayerfully read and ponder the scriptures to understand the meaning of life, the plan of salvation, the true nature of God, the Atonement, and life after death. Allow spiritual healing to teach you obedience, humility, compassion, and sensitivity to the promptings of the Spirit.

REMAIN HOPEFUL FOR THE PROMISES OF HEALING

Healing is truly the "divine gift always available from a loving Heavenly Father" and the "regenerating power [that] is with us today."[14] Continue to fill your mind with the words of the Savior and His prophets so that His peace and hope of a bright future will be manifested in your heart.

Furthermore, *expect* that as you respond to the Savior's call to follow Him, you will be given guidance and strength to obey His commandments and endure your challenges. Spiritual healing is nothing short of miraculous. As you strive to gain it, look for and record the miracles—all along your journey toward joy.

LEARN THE HEALER'S ART

When you have felt the light of the Savior's healing, "learn the healer's art" and "show a gentle heart" "to the wounded and the weary" (*Hymns,* 1985, no. 220).

President Gordon B. Hinckley has counseled that "ours is a ministry of healing, with a duty to bind the wounds and ease the pain of those who suffer."[15] Moreover, "every day someone in your path is hurting, someone is afraid, someone feels inadequate, or someone needs a friend. Someone needs you to notice, to reach out, and to help him or her to heal. You may not know who that is at the time, but you can give encouragement and hope. You can help heal wounds of misunderstanding and contention. You can serve 'in the cause of the Master Healer.'"[16]

May the Lord bless and strengthen all of us in our overwhelming yet divine tutorials of life.

Chapter 21

STRENGTHEN THY BRETHREN

*E*lder Neal A. Maxwell wrote: "When, for the moment, we ourselves are not being stretched on a particular cross, we ought to be at the foot of someone else's—full of empathy and proffering spiritual refreshment."[1] Being "willing to mourn with those that mourn" is an "obligation and [a] great gift,"[2] and we can learn to extend our hearts to those who suffer. The following ideas might by helpful in "strengthen[ing] thy brethren" (Luke 22:32) who are striving to heal.

REACH OUT TO THOSE WHO GRIEVE

Reaching out to those who suffer starts with awareness and acknowledgment. Acknowledge those who are suffering when you see them. Ignoring them or their challenges is a painful reminder of the loneliness they already feel. Make such statements as "It's good to see you," or "I've been thinking of you," as opposed to asking, "How are you doing?"—which implies they should give you an answer.[3]

Likewise, validate their loss by remembering those who have died ("I thought of your child today"), or by empathizing with their burden ("I'm sorry to hear about your loss," or "This must be so difficult to bear"). Validation of their loss may facilitate conversation if your loved ones want to talk.

As President Heber J. Grant discovered, we need to realize that "we are not able to lift from their shoulders the sorrow into which they are plunged, when they are called upon to part with those they cherish."[4] Instead, help to carry that weight by the power of your sincere prayers and acts of service. Make specific offers, such as "Can I baby-sit your children today?" or "Can I help with your laundry?" Or simply take care of tasks that need to be done, such as raking leaves or taking the garbage can out to the street.

LISTEN, LISTEN, LISTEN

Because it takes time to show others that you care, be available to spend time with your grieving loved ones, and seek the Spirit to know when it is appropriate to talk about their loss. Watch for verbal cues to understand whether your loved ones want to talk. Sometimes, the bereaved feel that discussing the loss only means reliving intense sorrow or feeling burdened to "endure an interview" just to help others feel better about the situation.

Ask sincere questions as the Spirit directs, and then listen carefully and strive for understanding. Allow your loved ones most of your time together to express their words, thoughts, and emotions—without worrying about your reactions or feelings. Suppress any urge to solve their problems or to take away their pain. Likewise, do not judge, blame, or condemn; do not criticize, gossip, or find fault.[5] Don't give trite answers or over-simplify problems and solutions by trying to explain their loss (for example, "Heavenly Father needed your child," or "It's better this way").

Respect your loved ones' feelings by allowing them to cry and to grieve. Do not become distracted or preoccupied with anything else, even your own past sorrow. At the same time, be "willing to mourn with those that mourn" (Mosiah 18:9) by feeling some pain—whether their pain or your own.

Let your loved ones determine their own solutions, and take no offense if they refute either your past way of grieving or your answers for healing. Every person's path of healing is individual, and each must come to his or her own conclusions and scriptural applications.

BE SENSITIVE AND SUPPORTIVE

Choose your words carefully. Without the Spirit, your words can inflict more damage; but with the Spirit, even using the same words, you can truly "understand one another, and both are edified and rejoice together" (D&C 50:22). Therefore, avoid phrases that aren't true, such as "I know how you feel" (no one's experiences are exactly the same as another's), or "Don't worry; you can always have another child" (which actually might be your own way of dealing with the death of their child).

Realize that when the funeral is over and the cards, flowers, and phone calls stop coming, "the loss becomes very real. The weeks and months that follow are more important than ever in remembering your grieving friend or loved one."[6]

Be sensitive to dates, anniversaries, and situations that are potentially painful (pregnancies, baby showers, baby blessings, Sundays, holidays, etc.). It is appropriate to extend gifts and notes to show your concern at these times. Continue to invite your friend or loved one to sit with you at church, attend family dinners and social gatherings, visit the cemetery, go to a movie, get an ice cream treat, or take a walk together.[7]

Likewise, be sensitive if you have a child the age of the deceased child; what your child does at a particular time might be a reminder of the painful void your loved one may be experiencing.

Above all, keep confidences, be an example of faith, quiet acceptance, forgiveness, and hope, and continue supporting, loving, and praying for your grieving loved one.

May the Lord bless you as you pray for inspiration to be of genuine help as you share your tears, warm hugs, and listening ear.

NOTES

Chapter 2

WHERE CAN I TURN FOR PEACE?

1. "Policies, Practices, and Procedures: Stillborn Children," in Ludlow, *Encyclopedia of Mormonism,* 3:1097.

2. Smith, *Doctrines of Salvation,* 2:280.

3. LDS Bible Dictionary, "Revelation," 762.

Chapter 3

SUCCOR IN OUR TIME OF NEED

1. Kimball, *Teachings of Spencer W. Kimball,* 252.

Chapter 4

FAITH TO LET GO

1. *Wilford Woodruff,* 223.

2. Kimball, *Faith Precedes the Miracle,* 99–100.

Chapter 5
THOU SHALT WEEP FOR THE LOSS OF THEM THAT DIE

1. Rando, *Grieving,* 19–26, 11–17.

2. Ibid., 17, 63–72.

3. See, for example, McCracken and Semel, *Broken Heart Still Beats.*

4. Rando, *Grieving,* 169.

Chapter 6
UNDERSTANDING DEVIN'S ETERNAL PROGRESSION

1. *Gospel Principles,* 10.

2. Ibid., 17.

3. Smith, *Teachings of the Prophet Joseph Smith,* 196–97.

4. Smith, *Doctrines of Salvation,* 2:56; Smith, *Gospel Doctrine,* 455; see also Crowther, *Life Everlasting,* for a comprehensive discussion of life after death.

5. McConkie, *Mormon Doctrine,* 755; see also Alma 40:13–14; *Gospel Principles,* 280.

6. McConkie, *Mormon Doctrine,* 674.

7. Heber C. Kimball, *Journal of Discourses,* 4:135.

8. Brigham Young, ibid., 17:142.

9. Dyer, *Who Am I?* 489.

10. *Gospel Principles,* 68; see also 1 Corinthians 15:21–22.

11. Smith, *Improvement Era,* June 1904, 623–24; see also Smith, *Gospel Doctrine,* 455–56.

12. In Smith, *Gospel Doctrine,* 453–54; see also discussion on nurturing children after the resurrection in Crowther, *Life Everlasting,* 252–56.

13. Smith, *Doctrines of Salvation,* 2:56.

14. *Gospel Principles,* 349; D&C 68:27.

15. See also the discussion of God's eternal plan for mentally disabled persons in Hill, *Angel Children,* 42–46.

16. Smith, *Doctrines of Salvation,* 2:55, 54, 55.

17. Ibid., 55.

18. Ballard, *Crusader for Righteousness,* 278.

Chapter 7

LEAD, KINDLY LIGHT, AMID TH' ENCIRCLING GLOOM

1. *Guide to the Scriptures,* retrieved Feb. 2, 2006, from http://scriptures. lds.org/en/gs/m/26; LDS Bible Dictionary, "Grace," 697.

Chapter 8

ANSWERS FROM ON HIGH

1. In "Lindbergh Nightmare," *Time,* Feb. 5, 1973, 35.

2. Frankl, *Man's Search for Meaning,* 60, 88.

3. Whitney, quoted in Kimball, *Faith Precedes the Miracle,* 98.

4. Lundwall, comp., *Lectures on Faith,* 3:4–5; Smith, *Teachings of the Prophet Joseph Smith,* 343.

5. Wheatley, "Honoring Our God-Given Gifts," 2.

6. Jacob, "Why Aren't I Happy?" *Ensign,* Jan. 1991, 68–69.

7. "A Refuge for the Oppressed," *Ensign,* Jan. 1992, 62–63.

8. Ibid., 64.

9. Jacob, "Why Aren't I Happy?" 69.

10. Wheatley, "Honoring Our God-Given Gifts," 5.

11. George Q. Cannon, "Freedom of the Saints," in *Collected Discourses,* 2:185, as quoted in Maxwell, *If Thou Endure It Well,* 121.

Chapter 10

WAITING UPON THE LORD

1. Hafen, *Believing Heart,* 86–89.

Chapter 11

INTO THE LIGHT OF HEALING

1. Hinckley, "Stand True and Faithful," *Ensign,* May 1996, 94.

Chapter 14

SWEET ABOVE ALL THAT IS SWEET

1. Faust, "Father, Come Home," *Ensign,* May 1993, 37; "Elijah, Spirit of," in Ludlow, *Encyclopedia of Mormonism,* 2:452.

2. McConkie, *New Witness for the Articles of Faith,* 185.

3. Ibid., 186.

4. LDS Bible Dictionary, "Atonement," 617.

5. "The Family: A Proclamation to the World," *Ensign,* Nov. 1995, 102.

Chapter 15

THANK THE LORD THY GOD IN ALL THINGS

1. Jarvik, "'Friends' Share the Grief Only a Parent Can Know," *Deseret News,* May 28, 2000, A1.

2. See Hafen, "The Atonement: All for All," *Ensign,* May 2004, 97–99.

3. Hales, "Gratitude for the Goodness of God," *Ensign,* May 1992, 64–65.

4. Ibid., 65; see also Faust, "Gratitude as a Saving Principle," *Ensign,* May 1990, 85.

5. LDS Bible Dictionary, "Eben-ezer," 659; see also 1 Samuel 7:12.

6. "Come, Thou Fount of Every Blessing," in Morgan, *Then Sings My Soul,* 64; see also *Hymns,* 1948, no. 70.

7. Hales, "Gratitude for the Goodness of God," 63.

8. Morgan, *Then Sings My Soul,* 64; see also *Hymns,* 1948, no. 70.

Chapter 16

FAITH, HOPE, AND CHARITY

1. Talmage, *Jesus the Christ,* 387–88; see also 1 Corinthians 13:11; 14:20.

Chapter 17

A NEW STANDARD IS SET

1. Thomas, "Understanding Our True Identity," *Ensign,* May 1998, 91.

2. Simmons, "But If Not . . . ," *Ensign,* May 2004, 75.

3. Stradling, "Between Faith and Charity: Some Thoughts on Hope," *Ensign,* July 1981, 29.

4. See *Guide to the Scriptures,* retrieved Oct. 27, 2004, from http://scriptures.lds.org/en/gs/h/44.

5. Stradling, "Between Faith and Charity," 28.

6. Linton, "Forgiving Heart," *Ensign,* Apr. 1993, 15.

Chapter 18

A LIFETIME OF TUTORIALS

1. Holland, *Quiet Heart,* 19.

2. Maxwell, *Even As I Am,* 42–43; see also Hafen, *Disciple's Life,* 544.

3. Whitney, quoted in Kimball, *Faith Precedes the Miracle,* 98.

Chapter 19

JOY COMETH IN THE MORNING

1. *Heber J. Grant,* 45.

Chapter 20

LOOK TO GOD AND LIVE AGAIN

1. Wickman, "But If Not," *Ensign,* Nov. 2002, 30.

2. Ibid., 31.

3. See Rando, *Grieving.*

4. Church, Chazin, and Ewald, *When a Baby Dies,* 18.

5. Ibid., 20.

6. Marshall, "Lessons on Healing," *Ensign,* Apr. 2004, 57, 58.

7. Ibid., 59.

8. Church, Chazin, and Ewald, *When a Baby Dies,* 23.

9. Holland, "Come unto Me," in *Speeches,* 189; emphasis altered.

10. Marshall, "Lessons on Healing," 60.

11. Wickman, "But If Not," 30.

12. Maxwell, "Endure It Well," *Ensign,* May 1990, 33, 34; see also Alma 29:3, 6.

13. Eyring, "In the Strength of the Lord," *Ensign,* May 2004, 17, 18, 19.

14. Marshall, "Lessons on Healing," 60; Hinckley, "Healing Power of Christ," *Ensign,* Nov. 1988, 59.

15. Hinckley, "Healing Power of Christ," 59.

16. Marshall, "Lessons on Healing," 60.

Chapter 21

STRENGTHEN THY BRETHREN

1. Maxwell, "Endure It Well," 34.

2. Marshall, "Lessons on Healing," 60.

3. See Campbell and Hogan, *What Can I Do? What Can I Say?*

4. *Heber J. Grant,* 45.

5. See Ashton, "Tongue Can Be a Sharp Sword," *Ensign,* May 1992, 18–20.

6. Campbell and Hogan, *What Can I Do? What Can I Say?* 18.

7. Ibid., 22–23.

SOURCES

BOOKS

Ballard, Melvin J. *Crusader for Righteousness.* Salt Lake City: Bookcraft, 1966.

Campbell, Kathi, and Julia Hogan. *What Can I Do? What Can I Say? More Than 150 Ways to Give Comfort to Those Who Mourn.* JKP Group, 2001.

Children's Songbook of The Church of Jesus Christ of Latter-day Saints. Salt Lake City: The Church of Jesus Christ of Latter-day Saints, 1989.

Church, Martha Jo, Helene Chazin, and Faith Ewald. *When a Baby Dies.* Oak Brook, Ill.: Compassionate Friends, 1981.

Collected Discourses. Compiled by Brian H. Stuy. 5 vols. Burbank, Calif.: B. H. Stuy Publishing, 1988.

Crowther, Duane S. *Life Everlasting.* Salt Lake City: Bookcraft, 1971.

Dyer, Alvin R. *Who Am I?* Salt Lake City: Deseret Book, 1966.

Frankl, Victor E. *Man's Search for Meaning.* New York: Washington Square Press, 1984.

Gospel Principles. Salt Lake City: The Church of Jesus Christ of Latter-day Saints, 1981.

Hafen, Bruce C. *The Believing Heart.* 2d ed. Salt Lake City: Deseret Book, 1990.

———. *A Disciple's Life: The Biography of Neal A. Maxwell.* Salt Lake City: Deseret Book, 2002.

Heber J. Grant. A volume in the series *Teachings of Presidents of the Church.* Salt Lake City: The Church of Jesus Christ of Latter-day Saints, 2002.

Hill, Mary V. *Angel Children: Those Who Die Before Accountability.* Bountiful, Utah: Horizon Publishers, 1973.

Holland, Jeffrey R. "Come unto Me." In *Brigham Young University 1996–97 Speeches.* Provo, Utah: Brigham Young University, 1997.

Holland, Patricia T. *A Quiet Heart.* Salt Lake City: Bookcraft, 2000.

Hymns. Salt Lake City: The Church of Jesus Christ of Latter-day Saints, 1948.

Hymns of The Church of Jesus Christ of Latter-day Saints. Salt Lake City: The Church of Jesus Christ of Latter-day Saints, 1985.

Journal of Discourses. 26 vols. London: Latter-day Saints' Book Depot, 1854–86.

Kimball, Spencer W. *Faith Precedes the Miracle.* Salt Lake City: Deseret Book, 1973.

———. *The Teachings of Spencer W. Kimball.* Edited by Edward W. Kimball. Salt Lake City: Bookcraft, 1982.

Ludlow, Daniel H., et al., eds. *Encyclopedia of Mormonism.* 4 vols. New York: Macmillan, 1992.

Lundwall, N. B., comp. *A Compilation Containing the Lectures on Faith.* Salt Lake City: Bookcraft, n.d.

Maxwell, Neal A. *Even As I Am.* Salt Lake City: Deseret Book, 1982.

———. *If Thou Endure It Well.* Salt Lake City: Bookcraft, 1996.

McConkie, Bruce R. *Mormon Doctrine.* 2d ed. Salt Lake City: Bookcraft, 1966.

———. *A New Witness for the Articles of Faith.* Salt Lake City: Deseret Book, 1985.

McCracken, Anne, and Mary Semel, eds. *A Broken Heart Still Beats: After Your Child Dies.* Center City, Minn.: Hazelden, 1998.

Morgan, Robert J. *Then Sings My Soul: 150 of the World's Greatest Hymn Stories.* Nashville: Thomas Nelson, 2003.

Rando, Theresa A. *Grieving: How to Go on Living When Someone You Love Dies.* Lexington, Mass.: Lexington Books, 1988.

Smith, Joseph. *Teachings of the Prophet Joseph Smith.* Selected by Joseph Fielding Smith. Salt Lake City: Deseret Book, 1978.

Smith, Joseph F. *Gospel Doctrine.* 5th ed. Salt Lake City: Deseret Book, 1963.

Smith, Joseph Fielding. *Doctrines of Salvation.* Compiled by Bruce R. McConkie. 3 vols. Salt Lake City: Bookcraft, 1954–56.

Talmage, James E. *Jesus the Christ.* Salt Lake City: Deseret Book, 1977.

Wilford Woodruff. A volume in the series *Teachings of Presidents of the Church.* Salt Lake City: The Church of Jesus Christ of Latter-day Saints, 2004.

ARTICLES AND ELECTRONIC MEDIA

Ashton, Marvin J. "The Tongue Can Be a Sharp Sword." *Ensign,* May 1992, 18.

Eyring, Henry B. "In the Strength of the Lord." *Ensign,* May 2004, 17.

"The Family: A Proclamation to the World." *Ensign,* Nov. 1995, 102.

Faust, James E. "Father, Come Home." *Ensign,* May 1993, 37.

———. "Gratitude as a Saving Principle." *Ensign,* May 1990, 85.

Guide to the Scriptures. The Church of Jesus Christ of Latter-day Saints (electronic media and online): scriptures.lds.org

Hafen, Bruce C. "The Atonement: All for All." *Ensign,* May 2004, 97.

Hales, Robert D. "Gratitude for the Goodness of God." *Ensign,* May 1992, 64.

Hinckley, Gordon B. "The Healing Power of Christ." *Ensign,* Nov. 1988, 59.

————. "Stand True and Faithful." *Ensign,* May 1996, 94.

Jacob, Jeffrey C. "Why Aren't I Happy?" *Ensign,* Jan. 1991, 68.

Jarvik, Elaine. "'Friends' Share the Grief Only a Parent Can Know." *Deseret News,* 28 May 2000, A1.

"Lindbergh Nightmare." *Time,* 5 Feb. 1973, 35.

Linton, Roderick J. "A Forgiving Heart." *Ensign,* Apr. 1993, 15.

Marshall, Elaine S. "Lessons on Healing." *Ensign,* Apr. 2004, 57.

Maxwell, Neal A. "Endure It Well." *Ensign,* May 1990, 34.

"A Refuge for the Oppressed." *Ensign,* Jan. 1992, 62.

Simmons, Dennis E. "But If Not . . ." *Ensign,* May 2004, 73.

Smith, Joseph F. "On the Resurrection." *Improvement Era,* June 1904, 623–24.

Stradling, Rebecca Gwynn. "Between Faith and Charity: Some Thoughts on Hope." *Ensign,* July 1981, 27.

Thomas, Carol B. "Understanding Our True Identity." *Ensign,* May 1988, 91.

Wheatley, Margaret P. "Honoring Our God-Given Gifts." Unpublished manuscript in author's possession.

Wickman, Lance B. "But If Not." *Ensign,* Nov. 2002, 30.

INDEX